Tangled Vines

Tangled Vines

A Collection of
Mother and Daughter
Poems

EDITED BY
LYN LIFSHIN

A HARVEST ORIGINAL

HARCOURT BRACE & COMPANY

San Diego   New York   London

Requests for permission to make copies
of any part of the work should be mailed to:
Permissions Department, Harcourt Brace & Company,
6277 Sea Harbor Drive, Orlando, Florida 32887-6777.

Library of Congress Cataloging-in-Publication Data
Tangled vines: a collection of mother and daughter poems/edited
    by Lin Lifshin. — 1st ed.
        p.   cm.
    ISBN 0-15-688166-7
    1. Mothers and daughters — Poetry.   2. American poetry —
Women authors.   3. American poetry — 20th century.
I. Lifshin, Lyn.
PS595.M65T3   1992
811.008'03520431   dc20   91-45028

Designed by Lydia D'moch

Printed in the United States of America

First edition
G F E D C B

Permission acknowledgments appear on pages 159–164 and
constitute a continuation of the copyright page.

Contents

Preface

Fifteen years ago I decided to work on an anthology of mother and daughter poems. I'd written almost nothing on the subject myself. I hadn't imagined conducting a mother and daughter workshop, what it would involve, or even why I would want to do one. (Now, it is the workshop I lead most often and enjoy the most.) Many of the excellent fiction and nonfiction collections dealing with the mother-daughter relationship had not yet been written, and of those available I'd read almost none.

But a number of poems on the subject fascinated me, especially some by Anne Sexton and Sylvia Plath that seemed their strongest work. I knew it was a relationship long ignored in patriarchal societies — in art and literature as well as in life. As Adrienne Rich writes in her chapter on motherhood and daughterhood in *Of Woman Born*, the mother-daughter relationship "has been minimized and trivialized. . . . Whether in theological doctrine or art or sociology or psychoanalytic theory, it is the mother and son who appear as the eternal, determinative dyad. Small wonder, since theology, art, and social theory have been produced by sons."

There was a special excitement and interest in discovering new insights into one another's lives in the women's movement, in understanding how internal and external events shape many relationships between women, especially this primary bond. If I was amazed in 1978, while writing the introduction to the first edition of *Tangled Vines*, at the range of experiences, the power, intensity, and ambivalence of the bond expressed in the manuscripts that came pouring into my mailbox, now, fourteen years later, I am even more astonished at the passion, electricity, difficulty, profound richness, and joy of this devastatingly fierce, strong connection.

Like other family ties, the mother and daughter bond is never easy or simple; there is so much intimacy, so many expectations and blends of pride and disappointment that collide. Perhaps it is from a combination of ambivalence and intensity as constantly changing and interconnected as patterns that touch, scatter, and touch again in a kaleidoscope, that such emotional rawness, that so many powerful feelings and poems emerge. Even when mothers and daughters are separated or estranged — in life or by death — there seems to be energy that is never casual, unimportant, or totally finished.

Much in this collection seems to have been written out of emotional necessity. Unlike sons and mothers, daughters and mothers do not see each other as "other" easily, and many daughters' poems suggest that seeing their mothers is like trying to see themselves pressed to glass. Often terror and rage grow from this vision. And mothers, who see what they were in their teenage daughters and sense they are being replaced, can experience conflicting feelings. In the most loving poems, there is apt to be a dark image, and in the most angry passages there is still a desire for a mother's approval and love.

Pain and joy abound in these poems along with longing, yearning, and an astounding tenacity. Photographs of mothers and daughters often share this same emotional tension. In some, the mother holds on to the daughter as if to prevent escape or cover up a hole inside herself. In others, the daughter could be a sign held up by a hitchhiker trying to get away. And in photographs as in the poems, we see sullenness, disgust, distaste, pride, playfulness, admiration, resentment, estrangement, communication. In *Tangled Vines*, little girls become adolescents, mature into women, grow old, and move away from and then toward their mothers. Sometimes that closeness is comforting and soothing; at other times it is like sandpaper.

There are secrets throughout these poems, the things mothers and daughters can never talk about: questions never asked, answers never given. In various phases of the relationship, many women seem haunted by questions of how to connect but not merge, respond but not be absorbed, be separate but not be isolated, hold but not hold on. There is the need for approval, the need to keep going back to get it right, as if that need were a hook that can't be spit out or swallowed.

Several of the poems deal with death: not only physical death but the deaths of stages in the relationship that start when the mother sees the infant as separate, and continue as the teenage daughter rebels and turns away, rejecting the mother. The mother watches her daughter leave home, then the adult daughter watches her mother age, become needy, and head toward a world the daughter can't fathom. In the tangle that nourishes and chokes, gives life to yet tethers, like an umbilical cord, the terrifying pull toward becoming one's mother is linked with a longing to be her. It's this tangle that makes the poems so fascinating: one strand seems to be working its way out as another starts reeling in, knotting, twisting, braiding, catching.

So much haunts the women in these poems: a mother looks ahead and worries as she sees her daughter in pain she cannot control and as she sees herself being replaced. A daughter looks back and sees her mother, a stranger in photographs — so youthful and optimistic, filled with possibilities. As her mother ages or becomes sick the adult daughter is haunted by the realization she cannot rescue or keep her mother.

Some mothers are haunted by the fear of being fairy godmothers or bad witches and worry that they have either bound their daughters' feet or sent them into danger. Some daughters feel that they were hobbled, others that they were never accepted for being what they were.

Taboos about mothers and sons, especially in terms of touching and intimacy, also exist for mothers and daughters. Yet these poems are very sensual, even erotic, and talk of bodies and touching. The joys and pleasures, as well as the difficulties, of holding and hugging, of being open and admiring of each other are recurring subjects. Often mothers and daughters find excuses to touch by combing hair, straightening a skirt, brushing off lint. In several poems, being sick is a luxury because it means at least the chance to stroke a forehead, to give a back rub, to offer physical attention.

Some themes in these poems were expected: the birth of a daughter, the death of a mother. A number of poems are about advice: a mother choosing hairstyles and clothes, or telling her daughter how to make a bed, how to live a life. Many of the poems deal with mother and daughter fights, from a four-year-old's tantrums to an aging mother's obstinacy.

Rooms are remembered here, especially kitchens, bedrooms, and bathrooms, where intimacies and rituals were shared. I found few poems about adoption but many about "missing" mothers and daughters, about miscarriages, rejections, and refusals to acknowledge each other on many levels.

I'm struck by the fresh, vivid images in this collection. There are many animal images: cats, fish, falcons, rabbits, spiders, horses, beetles, mice — even the "birth-room zoo." It is not a surprise that many poems mention food and cooking, but the strength of the imagery is notable: chewing, biting, kneading, devouring, reshaping, tearing, beating, squeezing, burning. There are also soft, sensuous images: fur, skin, lips, hands, lace, cotton, and lots of hair — hair that is combed, darkened, washed, held, twisted, and plaited. There are sewing images: hems, needles, threads, buttons, pockets, zippers, scissors, hooks and eyes. And there is a rich variety of smells: skin, powder, jam, lipstick, soap, perfume, soup, lilies, hyacinths, the scent of a mother's closet or a young girl's cotton.

Several poems concern gifts, apprenticeships, and inheritances. A newborn baby can be a gift, as can forgiveness and acceptance. A daughter can serve an apprenticeship with her mother — learning to make jam, make a bed, deal with men — or receive an inheritance, be it material, physical, or emotional. Some poems are about going through a mother's things as if excavating a city or going on a treasure hunt;

ghosts fill her clothes, holding her shape and smell and turn-
ing the ordinary magical.

In my introduction to the earlier edition of *Tangled Vines* I
wrote that I wanted to celebrate this relationship, that I
hoped "the subject would touch and intrigue people who
might not ordinarily read poetry." While editing my collec-
tion of women's diaries and journals, *Ariadne's Thread*, I kept
a journal up to the manuscript delivery date. On the last day,
a letter from someone who had just discovered *Tangled Vines*
came, saying, "My husband never browses in the poetry sec-
tion of the bookstore so I still can't figure out how we were
guided to your book. But I found him in a corner reading
with tears in his eyes. This is a man who doesn't do much
public crying. We bought the book and drove to the beach
where we read it to each other, sharing tears and old mother
stories. I thank you for such a wonderful experience."

I hope this expanded collection, with its strong and de-
lightful new poems, will touch and intrigue new and old
readers on this subject. Of my four anthologies, it's the first
whose growth I wasn't able to share with my mother.
Thoughts of her are never far from me, though, and, like so
much that I do, this book is in her memory, is for her.

Lyn Lifshin
Niskayuna, NY

Tangled Vines

Rachel
(Rachel [rā'chal], a ewe)

LINDA PASTAN

We named you
for the sake
of the syllables
and for the small boat
that followed the *Pequod*,
gathering lost children
of the sea.

We named you
for the dark-eyed girl
who waited at the well
while her lover
worked seven years
and again
seven.

We named you
for the small daughters
of the Holocaust
who followed their six-pointed stars
to death
and were all of them
known as
Rachel.

from *Three Women*

SYLVIA PLATH

I see her in my sleep, my red, terrible girl.
She is crying through the glass that separates us.
She is crying, and she is furious.
Her cries are hooks that catch and grate like cats.
It is by these hooks she climbs to my notice.
She is crying at the dark, or at the stars
That at such a distance from us shine and whirl.

I think her little head is carved in wood,
A red, hard wood, eyes shut and mouth wide open.
And from the open mouth issue sharp cries
Scratching at my sleep like arrows,
Scratching at my sleep, and entering my side.
My daughter has no teeth. Her mouth is wide.
It utters such dark sounds it cannot be good.

Her Sleep

JILL HOFFMAN

Wasps or hornets rattle on the sills
and fill the vestibule with danger;
my daughter, rocked by lullabies
of wind, naps inside mosquito netting
like a bride before the veil is lifted
for the rough world to injure with its kiss.
Still a wound my husband cannot enter
since the child departed from me — her dream
drags its belly, suns on a honeyed spoon —
seeing her sleep, I am stung.

Thoughts About My Daughter Before Sleep
SANDRA HOCHMAN

1
Ariel, one true
Miracle of my life, my golden
Sparrow, burning in your crib
As the rain falls over the meadow
And the squirrel corn,
While the fragrant hyacinth
Sleeps in its bed in the rich
Mud of the North, while foamflowers
Climb through small arches of rain, and the sun
Brings lilies and dark blue berries
In cluster, leaf on leaf again,
I wonder how I came to give you life.

2
Here, where the twisted stalks
Of deer grass zigzag
Branches from the tree, where
Honeysuckles trumpet, "All joy
Is in the dark vessels of the skin!"
And thorn apples open their leaves,
I marvel to have made you perfect
As a small plant, you, filled
Up with sunlight and
Fragrant as ferns.

3
And before snow
Covers ivy and bluet
Shall I teach you this old
Summer's lesson
About seeds? About miracles
Of growth? Here are the bursting zinnias,
Asters, prongs
Of phlox—shall I wake you?
Take you out of sleep
And roll you in the apple fields?

4
And through you
I am born as I lie down
In the seed box of my own beginnings,
Opening the wild part of me,
Once lost once lost
As I was breathing
In the vines of childhood.

To My Four-Year-Old Daughter
GAIL TODD

I lost my temper twice today,
Once when you ordered me around like a maid,
And once when you picked all the unripe plums from our
    tree.
You said I yelled so much it made you sleepy,
Popped in your thumb and drifted away.
Then, imagining you sad, I felt guilty.
You, my firstborn child, my beautiful girl.
Remember when your ear hurt and we rocked all night.
How many hours, awake, I stared in your face
Seeing prongs that reach
Deep in your childhood, deep in mine.

Forgiveness

ALICE WALKER

Each time I order her to go
for a ruler and face her small
grubby outstretched palm
i feel before hitting it
the sting in my own
and become my mother
preparing to chastise me
on a gloomy Saturday afternoon
long ago and glaring down into my own sad
and grieving face i forgive myself
for whatever crime i may
have done as i wish i could always
forgive myself
then as now.

Waiting for the Transformation
JUDITH MINTY

My daughter is a mystic about cats.
I am afraid. I have seen her conversing with them,
watched her nod, blink her eyes; and the cats
twitch their whiskers, almost smile.
When she was five, she told me that if our old Tom
curled close to the fire, there would be
snow the next day. Often there was.

I think, although I fear to know for certain,
that she becomes a cat at night.
Just yesterday, I saw tiger shadows
on the wall of her room. I hear strange cries
in the house before dawn, feel the rattle of purrs,
a softness that feathers my face.

I do not think about it, tell no one.
I have decided to wait until other children's eyes
glint fire, until they all leave their mothers' arms
and turn wild—howling in the night.

My Daughter's Ring
BARBARA EVE

A ring of fear
through the nose
yanks her from a dream,
pulls her to the bathroom
mirror where she sees
a thin silver wire
piercing her nostrils,
its metallic perfume
jolting her like ammonia,
as invisible threads
shoot from the ring,
slip down her throat
and wind around her stomach
tighter, tighter,
until she bends
in the sick smell of night
to vomit, sensing,
even at six,
that the ring will grow
as she grows
and will always fit — perfectly.

What My Child Learns of the Sea

AUDRE LORDE

What my child learns of the sea
of the summer thunders
of the riddles that hide in the curve of spring
she will learn in my twilights
and childlike
revise every autumn

What my child learns
as her winters grow into time
has ripened in my own body
to enter her eyes with first light

This is why
more than blood
or the milk I have given
one day a strange girl will step
to the back of a mirror
cutting my ropes
of sea and thunder and spring.
Of the way she will taste her autumns—
toast-brittle or warmer than sleep—
and the words she will use for winter
I stand already condemned

Mothers, Daughters
SHIRLEY KAUFMAN

Through every night we hate,
preparing the next day's
war. She bangs the door.
Her face laps up my own
despair, the sour, brown eyes,
the heavy hair she won't
tie back. She's cruel,
as if my private meanness
found a way to punish us.
We gnaw at each other's
skulls. Give me what's mine.
I'd haul her back, choking
myself in her, herself
in me. There is a book
called *Poisons* on her shelf.
Her room stinks with incense,
animal turds, hamsters
she strokes like silk. They
exercise on the bathroom
floor, and two drop through
the furnace vent. The whole
house smells of the accident,
the hot skins, the small
flesh rotting. Six days
we turn the gas up then
to fry the dead. I'd fry
her head if I could until
she cried, Love, love me!
All she won't let me do.

Her stringy figure in
the windowed room shares
its thin bones with no one.
Only her shadow on the glass
waits like an older sister.
Now she stalks, leans forward,
concentrates merely on getting
from here to there. Her feet
are bare. I hear her breathe
where I can't get in. If I
break through to her, she will
drive nails into my tongue.

Aubade
LINDA PASTAN

In the early morning
I shake my head
to clear away the static
of the dream
the way my daughter
shakes the radio she holds
against her ear
as if it were a shell.
On the table between us
the sun spreads
its slow stain;
fog lifts
from the coffee;
a heart drifts out of reach
on the surface
of the milk.
Now my daughter takes the day
into her hand
like fresh-baked bread —
she offers me a piece.

Pajamas
SHARON OLDS

My daughter's pajamas lie on the floor
inside out, thin and wrinkled as
peeled skins of peaches when you ease the
whole skin off at once.
You can see where her waist emerged, and her legs,
her arms, and head, the fine material
gathered in rumples like skin the caterpillar
ramped out of and left to shrivel.
You can see, there at the center of the bottoms,
the raised cotton seam like the line
down the center of fruit, where the skin first splits
and curls back. You can almost see the hard
halves of her young buttocks, the precise
stem-mark of her sex. Her shed
skin shines at my feet, and in the air there is a
sharp fragrance like peach brandy —
the birth-room pungence of her released life.

Pain for a Daughter
ANNE SEXTON

Blind with love, my daughter
has cried nightly for horses,
those long-necked marchers and churners
that she has mastered, any and all,
reining them in like a circus hand—
the excitable muscles and the ripe neck;
tending, this summer, a pony and a foal.
She who is too squeamish to pull
a thorn from the dog's paw
watched her pony blossom with distemper,
the underside of the jaw swelling
like an enormous grape.
Gritting her teeth with love,
she drained the boil and scoured it
with hydrogen peroxide until pus
ran like milk on the barn floor.

Blind with loss all winter,
in dungarees, a ski jacket, and a hard hat,
she visits the neighbors' stable,
our acreage not zoned for barns;
they who own the flaming horses
and the swan-whipped thoroughbred
that she tugs at and cajoles,
thinking it will burn like a furnace
under her small-hipped English seat.

Blind with pain she limps home.
The thoroughbred has stood on her foot.

He rested there like a building.
He grew into her foot until they were one.
The marks of the horseshoes printed
into her flesh, the tips of her toes
ripped off like pieces of leather,
three toenails swirled like shells
and left to float in blood in her riding boot.

Blind with fear, she sits on the toilet,
her foot balanced over the washbasin,
her father, hydrogen peroxide in hand,
performing the rites of the cleansing.
She bites on a towel, sucked-in breath,
sucked-in and arched against the pain,
her eyes glancing off me where
I stand at the door, eyes locked
on the ceiling, eyes of a stranger,
and then she cries . . .
Oh my God, help me!
Where a child would have cried *Mama!*
Where a child would have believed *Mama!*
she bit the towel and called on God
and I saw her life stretch out. . . .
I saw her torn in childbirth,
and I saw her, at that moment,
in her own death and I knew that she
knew.

For My Daughter
SHARON OLDS

That night will come. Somewhere someone will be
entering you, his body riding
under your white body, dividing
your blood from your skin, your dark, liquid
eyes open or closed, the slipping
silken hair of your head fine
as water poured at night, the delicate
threads between your legs curled
like stitches broken. The center of your body
will tear open, as a woman will rip the
seam of her skirt so she can run. It will happen,
and when it happens I will be right here
in bed with your father, as when you learned to read
you would go off and read in your room
as I read in mine, versions of the story
that changes in the telling, the story of the river.

For My Daughter
Ashley's 25th Birthday
CAROLYN KIZER

It was lingering summer
when you announced your birth,
as you were rapt in me,
rapt in a field-flower haze
of those last, listless days
the waters burst
in a summer storm:
Like Beethoven
your bold overture began.

It was sterile winter
in the birth-room zoo;
animals clung to the bars,
humped and yelled
as the fogs blew
through our primate skulls.
From a far-distant self
I dreamily overheard
the worst, visceral howl.

Eyes opened to autumn
overnight: the trees
red against blazing blue
framed by a lutheran wall.
You were brought in to me
so pitiably small
and unbelievably red
as if god had dyed

the leaves and you
with the same mercurochrome.

Your young new parents,
terrified,
held on to one another
as they cried.
Later, your father
returned, with a stern smile,
handed me gold chrysanthemums
wrapt in damp newspaper
smelling of earth and death
and man-inflicted pain.
I held my breath that night
to the light sound of rain
and prayed you to grow.

From that time, you took
each season in your stride.
Still, when an ideal passion
for man or justice seizes
your fierce imagination
that birth-day glow is kindled
on your cheek and brow.

Now, as you have reached
your quarter century,
with that same pristine fear
and undiminished pride
I thank your star, and you.

Letter to Jeanne (at Tassajara)

DIANE DI PRIMA

dry heat of the Tassajara canyon
moist warmth of San Francisco summer
bright fog reflecting sunrise as you
step out of September zendo
heart of your warmth, my girl, as you step out
into your vajra pathway, glinting
like your eyes turned sideways at us
your high knowing 13-year-old
wench-smile, flicking your thin
ankles you trot toward Adventure
all sizes and shapes, O may it be various
for you as for me it was, sparkle
like dust motes at dawn in the back
of grey stores, like the shooting stars
over the Hudson, wind in the Berkshire pines

O you have landscapes dramatic like mine
never was, uncounted caves
to mate in, my scorpio, bright love
like fire light up your beauty years
on these new, jagged hills

Letters to My Daughters #3

JUDITH MINTY

Your great-grandfather dreamed that his son
would be an engineer, the old man,
the blacksmith with square hands.
To the Finns up north in that snow country
engineer was like doctor today. In the forties
in Detroit, I learned to play the violin.
So did my father when he was a boy in Ishpeming.
He and I never spoke about becoming. Our conversation
was my bow slipping over the strings, my fingers
searching for notes to tell him, his foot tapping time.
That violin cracked ten years ago, it dried out
from loneliness in the coat closet.
Your grandfather, the engineer, sometimes plays his
at night behind a closed kitchen door.
Your grandmother sews and turns up the television.
But what of you two? The piano you practiced over
is still here, a deaf-mute in our living room.
I strike an imperfect chord now and remember
we never spoke of what was dreamed for you.

The One Girl at the Boys' Party
SHARON OLDS

When I take my girl to the swimming party
I set her down among the boys. They tower and
bristle, she stands there smooth and sleek,
her math scores unfolding in the air around her.
They will strip to their suits, her body hard and
indivisible as a prime number,
they'll plunge in the deep end, she'll subtract
her height from ten feet, divide it into
hundreds of gallons of water, the numbers
bouncing in her mind like molecules of chlorine
in the bright blue pool. When they climb out,
her ponytail will hang its pencil lead
down her back, her narrow silk suit
with hamburgers and french fries printed on it
will glisten in the brilliant air, and they will
see her sweet face, solemn and
sealed, a factor of one, and she will
see their eyes, two each,
their legs, two each, and the curves of their sexes,
one each, and in her head she'll be doing her
wild multiplying, as the drops
sparkle and fall to the power of a thousand from her body.

Circus Song

for Susan and Valerie Beere

PATRICIA GOEDICKE

Dear, you are in my hands like dough. Twisting
And turning, how
Can I get you free of me?

In the muffled agony of the pillow
Face down, beating it,
I know

For every step forward you take
Three backward and blame me.

Little yeasty thing
You call me animal trainer, insist

I keep you in the same cage
I'm trying to get you out of:

Talking all day long,
Backwards and forwards you keep pacing

Like a hungry cat in a circus
Over my bones you crack the whip

And then weep for it, the guilt
Just sticky enough to keep you

Right where you want to be, trapped,
Trying out your weapons but safe,
Wrapped in your warm coverings until you rise.

Dear clown, dear savage daughter
So different from me and yet
So much like me I know

No matter how much it hurts
Sharpening your claws on me first
Is how you begin to grow.

Listen
ALICIA OSTRIKER

Having lost you, I attract substitutes.
The student poets visit, think me wise,
Think me generous, confide in me.
Earnestly they sit in my office
Showing me their stigmata
Under the Judy Chicago poster
Of her half-opened writhing-petalled
Clitoris that appears to wheel
Slowly clockwise when you gaze at it,
And I sympathize. Then they try on their ambitions
Like stiff new hiking boots, and I laugh
And approve, telling them where to climb.
They bring me tiny plastic bags
Of healthy seeds and nuts, they bring me wine,
We huddle by the electric heater
When it is snowing,
We watch the sparrows dash
And when they leave we hug.

Oh silly mother, I can hear you mock.
Listen, loveliest, I am not unaware
This is as it must be.
Do daughters mock their mothers? Is Paris
A city? Do your pouring hormones
Cause you to do the slam
And other Dionysiac dances,
And did not even Sappho tear her hair
And act undignified, when the maiden
She wanted, the girl with the soft lips,

The one who could dance,
Deserted her?
Do I suffer? Of course I do,
I am supposed to, but listen, loveliest.
I want to be a shrub, you a tree.
I hum inaudibly and want you
To sing arias. I want to lie down
At the foot of your mountain
And rub the two dimes in my pocket
Together, while you dispense treasure
To the needy. I want the gods
Who have eluded me
All my life, or whom I have eluded,
To invite you regularly
To their lunches and jazz recitals.
Moreover I wish to stand on the dock
All by myself waving a handkerchief,
And you to be the flagship
Sailing from the midnight harbor,
A blue moon leading you outward,
So huge, so public, so disappearing—

I beg and beg, loveliest, I can't
Seem to help myself,
While you quiver and pull
Back, and try to hide, try to be
Invisible, like a sensitive
Irritated sea animal
Caught in a tide pool, caught
Under my hand, can I
Cut off my hand for you,
Cut off my life.

The Mountain
SHIRLEY KAUFMAN

1
In the morning I am alone in the icy room
everyone has gone to climb the mountain
the only sound is the noise in my head
machine of my anger or my fear
that won't shut off
the wind keeps cranking it.

My daughter has fled to the mountain
a piece of her dress in my hand
it is green
and I hold it next to my ear
to stop the wind.

What she took out of me
was not what I meant to give.
She hears strange voices.
I dream she's the child I grew up with
kneeling beside her hamsters
soft things she cared for
cradling them in her hands.

I want to make my words into a hamster
and nest them in her palms
to be sorry again
when she falls out of the tree
and breaks her arms.

She runs to an empty house
with her own prophets
they sit shoulder to shoulder
waiting for the sky to open
they can already see through a tiny crack
where the path begins.

2
Yesterday we saw how roots of mangroves
suck the warm sea at the desert's edge
and keep the salt
the leaves are white
and flaky as dead skin.
My ankles swell.
I must be drowning in my own brine.

A Bedouin woman stands veiled
in the ruined courtyard
there's a well
a hole in the ground
where she leads the camel by a rope
I watch her fill the bucket
and the camel drinks
lifting its small shrewd head
rinsing its teeth with a swollen tongue.

The woman is covered in black
her body her head her whole face black
except for the skin around her eyes.

My daughter watches me watch her
with the same eyes.

She picks up a handful of rocks
and hits the camel
shrieking she strikes it
over and over to make it move.

I am alone in the icy room
everyone has gone to climb the mountain
the only sound is the woman
chasing the camel with the rocks.

I look out at the dry riverbed.
I let her go.

Making the Jam Without You
for Judy

MAXINE KUMIN

Old daughter, small traveler
asleep in a German featherbed
under the eaves in a postcard town
of turrets and towers,
I am putting a dream in your head.

Listen! Here it is afternoon.
The rain comes down like bullets.
I stand in the kitchen,
that harem of good smells
where we have bumped hips and
cracked the cupboards with our talk
while the stove top danced with pots
and it was not clear who did
the mothering. Now I am
crushing blackberries
to make the annual jam
in a white cocoon of steam.

Take it, my sleeper. Redo it
in any of your three
languages and nineteen years.
Change the geography.
Let there be a mountain,
the fat cows on it belled
like a cathedral. Let
there be someone beside you
as you come upon the ruins

of a schloss, all overgrown
with a glorious thicket,
its brambles soft as wool.
Let him bring the buckets
crooked on his angel arms
and may the berries, vaster
than any forage in
the mild hills of New Hampshire,
drop in your pail, plum size,
heavy as the eyes
of an honest dog
and may you bear them
home together to a square
white unreconstructed kitchen
not unlike this one.

Now may your two heads
touch over the kettle,
over the blood of the berries
that drink up sugar and sun,
over that tar-thick boil
love cannot stir down.
More plainly than
the bric-a-brac of shelves
filling with jelly glasses,
more surely than
the light driving through them
trite as rubies, I see him
as pale as paraffin beside you.
I see you cutting
fresh-baked bread to spread it
with the bright royal fur.

At this time
I lift the flap of your dream
and slip out thinner than a sliver
as your two mouths open
for the sweet stain of purple.

Scenario
BARBARA EVE

My parents stand by my bed.
They look down, talking
about how I am growing before their eyes.

They watch as my hair
darkens and curls, as my milk teeth
fall out and new ones appear.

They barely blink when the rings
of my nipples rise like blown bubbles
and soft hair tops the vee of my legs.

They step back when a boy
joins me in bed and we kiss,
touching with tentative fingers.

They stand in the doorway
as the boy grows into a man and we kiss
harder, our bodies twisting into a braid.

They stare from the hallway
as my belly swells like a blister.
They fade back when I start labor.

I stand by her bed
seeing her grow before my eyes.
I step back.

A *Question of Time*
ALICIA OSTRIKER

I ask a friend. She informs me it is ten years
From when her mother wrote,
"I hope at least you are sorry
For causing your father's heart attack,"
To now, when they are speaking
Weekly on the phone
And almost, even, waxing confidential.
I check my watch. Ten years is rather much,
But I am not a Texas Fundamentalist,
And you are not a red-haired Lesbian,
So it should take us shorter, and I should get
Time off for good behavior
If I behave well, which
I do not plan to do.
No, on the contrary, I plan to play
All my cards wrong,
To pelt you with letters, gifts, advice,
Descriptions of my feelings.
I plan to ask friendly maternal questions.
I plan to beam a steady
Stream of anxiety,
Rays which would stun a mule,
Derail a train,
Take out a satellite,
At you in California, where you hack
Coldly away at this iron umbilicus,
Having sensibly put three thousand miles between us.
I remember you told me once, when we were still
In love, the summer before you left

For the hills of San Francisco,
The music of youth,
To stop fearing estrangement:
"Mom, you're not crazy like Grandma."
It was the country. We were on the balcony
Overlooking the pond, where your wiry boyfriend
And the rest of the family swam and drank, unconscious.
False but endearing, dear. I *am* my mother.
I am your mother. Are you keeping up
Your drawing, your reading?
Have you written poems?
Are you saving money? Don't
Do acid, it fries the brain,
Don't do cocaine, don't
Get pregnant, or have you already,
Don't slip away from me,
You said you wouldn't,
Remember that. I remember it was hot,
How lightly we were dressed,
And barefoot, at that time,
And how you let me rest
A half a minute in your suntanned arms.

from *Changing*
LIV ULLMANN

I was born in a small hospital in Tokyo. Mamma says she remembers two things:

A mouse running across the floor, which she took as a sign of good luck.

A nurse bending down and whispering apologetically: "I'm afraid it's a girl. Would you prefer to inform your husband yourself?"

The Petals of the Tulips
JUDITH HEMSCHEMEYER

The petals of the tulips
just before they open

when they're pulling
the last dark purple energy through the stem

are covered with a whitish veil,
a caul.

I like them best then:

they're me the month before I was born

the month Mother spent
flat on her back in the hospital.

The way I found out—

once, in round eight of one of our fights
I hissed at her, "I didn't ask to be born!"

and she threw back her head and howled,
remembering,

"You? You?

Hot as it was that summer
I had to lie there for weeks
hanging on to you.

You? You were begging to be born!"

The Second Heart
ELLEN WITTLINGER

The child I do not have
is the one my mother
always wanted. Every holiday
she asks what I have named it.

This child is like no other;
it will not hide in my belly
like a lodged bullet, pulling
the walls down around it.

It will not flower
in my mouth or cling
like a barnacle to my wooden
hip. It will not be my gift.

We will not speak of miracles.
We will not lay your head
on my lap listening
for my second heartbeat

that is half yours.
There will be no paper-doll
connections to send electricity
through the family.

But the child I do not have
will not be forgotten.
It hangs around my neck,
a heavy locket,

protecting me. I hear it
crying from a place inside
and I speak in tongues
only my mother understands.

It knows how old I am.
Each birthday now
I take away one candle
for the baby.

And you see the secret
in my hands, how they shake
when I undress,
when I make up the bed.

The child I do not have
rides on your shoulders
when we go out walking.
Everyone we pass notices.

Flowers

KATHLEEN FRASER

Changing water. Adding aspirin. Nitrogen, potash or
sugar (white) to keep limpness from descending
upon these purple and magenta asters with broad golden
    centers
and petals packed in two rows making fringe above
green spread leaves, still alive. Keep cutting stems
to retain the vertical pull of water up into
the barely charged life.

She said there was a tiny charge of energy still, like a cord,
    moving between
me and the child—a girl—though its body life had
    stopped after four months,
only one leg intact on the fetus. "It's better," the doctor
    said. "Nature
knows best," he said, at the end.

That was ten years ago. He was pulling me along on an
    immaculate silver table,
larger than a serving tray, I thought, sheet over me then,
    white linen, and
their faces soothing. Shapes of words and eyes. I couldn't
    identify. Something
inside me had broken, though I tried to hold it in. Red,
    on everything.

In the white stone pitcher I always place flowers.
First water, then the spiked metal frog
where each flower is stuck in arrangements of

height, darkness or intensity of bloom. The accidents
interest me. The Japanese effect of less.
Space showing its wandering shape between leaves
and the sudden curve of a stem
dying slowly towards what light is
in the room. One forgets about hunger,
absorbed in the fuchsia and the mauve.

For My Mother's Mother

JUDITH McDANIEL

Driving with my mother
from Chicago to Boston,
only ourselves to talk to.
In a snowstorm between Buffalo and Syracuse
she told me quietly
how her mother died.

I was eight and Lorraine was four.
Lorraine was a difficult child.
We moved a lot because of Daddy's job
but he had finally promised Mother they would settle.
They built a home in the country
with window seats and flagstone fireplace.
We moved in.
Three weeks later Daddy's company wanted him to move
    again.
He went.
Mother was going to pack and follow.
But Lorraine was a difficult child
and Mother was pregnant again.
She couldn't face moving and having another child
so she went to her mother and aunt.
Grandma Andersen told her something,
gave her something,
I don't know,
from the old country.
It didn't work.
She was sick.
I heard her screams from the next room

but they wouldn't let me go in.
By the time Daddy got home she was dead.

He never knew what happened or how she died.
What do you mean, I asked?
How could he not know?
Didn't he care? Didn't he ask?
They just told him it was a woman's problem.
He never knew. After he died
Grandma Andersen told Lorraine and she told me.
All I remembered was the house
where my mother died
and how she cried
and they finally took Lorraine and me away
so we wouldn't hear.

For two years now
I have heard my mother's mother's screams.
They are all I know of her;
they are with me.
I have listened to her screams
as they became my own.
I have lived through her death.
Untold, yet I know how she did it.
She took some poison
when that didn't work
she shoved something up her vagina.
And that worked and she bled
and expelled and was infected
and poisoned and she died.
I have heard her screams of pain
splutter through her clenched teeth

and grow weaker.
I have heard her screams of rage
deep in my chest.
as she cursed her husband
and her mother
and Lorraine who was always a difficult child
and herself who could not cope,
who should have been different
or better
or more able to manage these things somehow.

I asked, a year later: What was her name?
Whose?
Your mother, my grandmother,
what was her name?
Judith, she said.
I named my first daughter after my mother.

from Good Times
LUCILLE CLIFTON

My Mama moved among the days
like a dreamwalker in a field;
seemed like what she touched was hers
seemed like what touched her couldn't hold,
she got us almost through the high grass
then seemed like she turned around and ran
right back in
right back on in

For My Mother
ELLEN BASS

I am afraid to begin this poem.
I take a walk to the mailbox. I make a cup of tea.
I call opening lines into my head. None have power.
All the poems I've written of Dad, Herb, lovers—
and you, the one person I trust to love me, to be there
    for me, as long as you live, you, I don't know how to
    write to.

There is so much I could say to you, so much I feel for
    you,
so intimately my life is bound with yours, my life is yours,
this way we go beyond time, this way we are all of who we
    have been, will be, at once.
I think of Anne Sexton's words: "A woman *is* her mother.
                            That's the main thing."

I am you.
And so, there is nothing I can say about my feelings for
    you, nothing I can think of you that's simple.
Too closely am I mixed with everything I see.

Sometimes I look in the mirror and see in my mouth the
    same taut line I saw in yours
the day I came home and said I was going to Canada with
    a man.
I will never forget the way you stood, washing dishes,
    placing them on the soft towel,
crying and telling me all day you'd been counting out

wrong change for the customers, you'd buttoned your
sweater askew.
I went to the bathroom and brought you back Kleenex, a
pale gray-green Kleenex.
"With a strange man," you kept repeating.
I told you I wouldn't go and went secretly.

I find myself leaning my head on my hand, watching to
see if someone will walk through the gate.
I don't want to be disturbed.
The thread I feel between this flow of words and me is
tenuous, anything could break it, and so much I want
to say these things.

Our bodies — we have the same full breasts, the same well-
shaped legs, even at sixty you have well-shaped legs.
The same potbelly, small hips, pelvis tilted back,
protecting our sex.
Every morning I do yoga now. I do back bends. I rotate my
hips, listening to the bones crack into unfamiliar
positions.
I am trying to break our structure, to stop walking with my
chin thrust forward, my shoulders hunched up to my
ears — how you always admired long graceful necks.
Is it possible? Is it possible that years from now my body
will look less like yours?
How much leeway do I have to become myself?

Mother, there have been times when I've looked at your
marriage with Dad and I've thought you wasted
yourself,

you would've been happier with a man more full of joy,
 not a sick man,
someone who would've taught you the lindy, taken you
 sailing in a panama, pinched your behind while you
 scrambled the eggs.
And sometimes I've thought you beat him down, out-
 talked him, out-worked him, out-loved him till he just
 stopped trying.

And mostly, I know none of this is true, or it's all true, but
 so is everything else,
and I'm just afraid of the ways I'll choose my own life, the
 limits I'll set, the habits I won't give up.

Can you understand this? Is it too painful to read?
Last year when I gave you my book, you told me you
 weren't ready to talk about it.
Can we never talk about these things?
Oh, when Alan and I had stopped making love and I
 turned the living room upside down at least a couple
 times a week, crawled under the covers and screamed
 until he'd drive away, leaving Sunshine confused on the
 porch—
Mother, I wanted to call you and say, "Did this happen to
 you? Did you live through it? What is it in me—you
 know me—what is it that's making me like this, what is
 it I bring on myself?"
Am I so afraid my life will be like I imagine yours—warm,
 but not sexual; caring, but without passion?
Am I so afraid that I'm making it happen like that for
 myself?

Or are the patterns too strong to break anyway?
Tell me I'm wrong. Tell me you loved to make love.
Tell me I don't have to be afraid at how much I'm like
    you.

Oh Mother, when I think of you reading this, I feel
    wrong.
What right do I have to drag you through all my struggles?
And besides, you've been through your own. Isn't once
    enough?
With the sun shining on the wet bark of the redwoods and
    Sunshine biting at his fleas,
with the avocado growing like a beanstalk, not even I feel
    like wading through it all.
Sometimes I think I think too much.

The coils of my heater, glowing like a jack-o'-lantern,
    remind me of something you once said.
It was one of those days when I was 12 or 13 and combing
    my hair in the powder-room mirror, crying at the big
    mass of frizz, so unlike Judy Lockitch's silky flip.
Usually at times like this you knew enough to stay out of
    the way, knew anything you said would only make it
    worse,
but that day you must've had a clue that I needed
    something, needed you, and you said, "You won't
    always feel like this. Someday it won't matter."
I stopped crying and looked at you. "When?"
"I don't know," you told me, "but someday you won't care
    that you have curly hair."
I believed you. You were right.

I believed everything you said. I almost always obeyed.

Except around sex, which I hid, as I thought I sensed you ask me to.

That was the only place I cut myself away.

But I needed you—

with my recurrent cystitis and my mounting fear of that burning pee nothing seemed to cure for long,

with the knife-happy doctor in Baltimore who wouldn't even come to the emergency room when I was carried in—tubes clotted and about to burst—by a nice man passing by the hospital,

with the hometown boy returned from war who passed me gonorrhea in the front seat of his parents' car, hoping to give me a baby, even if I *was* on the pill—because he loved me so much (but not enough to drop a postcard telling me to check for clap). I carried *that* baby six months before I knew.

Momma, I began to think I really was sickly.

Momma, I needed to talk to you.

Momma—I've never called you Momma.

Mommy, when I was little. Mom, and Mother.

Who is this Momma arising here? this woman I could have talked to.

Does it sound like I'm accusing you?

Of course. And yet, I don't feel accusing at all right now. I don't even feel critical.

I'm not afraid today of being like you. I like you.

It's good to talk to you. Even if this hurts you, it's good to talk to you.

I don't think, deep down, you really want to be estranged
from me, really want me to keep so much to myself.
At least not all the time, not without the door opening
once in a while and the closed-off words rushing out.
Or, if you really don't want to know, then you're going to
have to tell me right out.
I'm not going to keep assuming it. I might be wrong.

What more is there to say?
Already the sun is going behind the trees.
This summer I thought you might be dying.
None of this made much difference then.
I remember the Wednesday I called you to get the first
word from the doctor.
Friends were here for the afternoon. We were down by the
river, skipping stones.
At five I came back to the house and called.
When I heard the good news — even that tentative good
news — I ran to the river calling out, "She's going to be
okay. It's okay."
Everyone was glad and they asked some questions, then
seemed to forget.
I returned to the house just to sit with the news, sit with
you, for a blissful while, giving thanks.

Oh Mom, live a long time. At least as long as Grandmom,
longer if you can and keep your health.
We're building a community here. A place with lots of
room.
Somewhere you could even live if you ever can't make
meals for yourself or do your little bit of cleaning up.

But that's a long way off. I only wanted to let you know I
won't forget you.

After saying all these hard things, there's a voice in me
urging, "Tell her about the good things. Tell her what
you appreciate."
And I could go on and on about the way you let me make
my own decisions, run my own affairs, never were
stupid like Marilyn's mother, telling her she couldn't
take art,
the way you never minded if I left my shoes in the living
room and you washed out my stockings just to do
for me.
You let me go to the beauty parlor with the other girls
even though you knew it was too soon,
and you never set much stock in getting rich, or being first
in the class, or famous,
never made me have table manners, say please or thank
you, just to look good, or go to synagogue, or say that I
believed in God.
And I remember how you held me and called him a
bastard when the delivery man forced his tongue into
my child mouth,
and the time I couldn't go to Girl Scout camp you let me
spend the whole ten dollars *any* way I wanted. I bought
a doll dress for $7.50 — and that was 1956.

When it snowed, you shoveled out the car, and you could
drive like a trucker and swing cases of beer onto the
counter.

All the customers loved you. The old caddy Roger called
    you Mom and held up his huge fist, showing over and
    over what he'd do if anybody ever tried to hurt you.
And you had the guts to play the numbers, the horses, and
    the stock market—I remember how you held Sunshine
    Mining for years because you liked the name.

But most of all is the way you loved me, loved me like I
    want to love and rarely can,
loved me with the feeling that nothing I could ever do,
                    no way I could ever be,
                        nothing that might happen in this world
could lessen, could change, how much you love me.

I am crying as I write this, Momma.
This time the Momma sounds right.
It is my grown-up woman's way of saying Mommy, my
    name of endearment,
to tell you I am grateful for how much you have loved me,
        I am grateful that through your love, you taught
        me love, and I am grateful to have this feeling
        welling up in me,
Mother, Mommy, Momma, Mom—I love you.

The Intruder
CAROLYN KIZER

My mother—preferring the strange to the tame:
Dove-note, bone marrow, deer dung,
Frog's belly distended with finny young,
Leaf-mould wilderness, hare-bell, toadstool,
Odd, small snakes roving through the leaves,
Metallic beetles rambling over stones: all
Wild and natural!—flashed out her instinctive love, and
  quick, she
Picked up the fluttering, bleeding bat the cat laid at her
  feet,
And held the little horror to the mirror, where
He gazed on himself, and shrieked like an old screen door
  far off.

Depended from her pinched thumb, each wing
Came clattering down like a small black shutter.
Still tranquil, she began, "It's rather sweet. . . ."
The soft mouse body, the hard feral glint
In the caught eyes. Then we saw,
And recoiled: lice, pallid, yellow,
Nested within the wing-pits, cosily sucked and snoozed.
The thing dropped from her hands, and with its thud,
Swiftly, the cat, with a clean careful mouth
Closed on the soiled webs, growling, took them out to the
  back stoop.

But still, dark blood, a sticky puddle on the floor
Remained, of all my mother's tender, wounding passion

For a whole wild, lost, betrayed and secret life
Among its dens and burrows, its clean stones,
Whose denizens can turn upon the world
With spitting tongue, an odor, talon, claw,
To sting or soil benevolence, alien
As our clumsy traps, our random scatter of shot.
She swept to the kitchen. Turning on the tap,
She washed and washed the pity from her hands.

My Mother Tries to Visit Me in the Dead of Night
DIANE WAKOSKI

I turn on all the lights.
I am never without electricity.
There was a girl who found a branch
from an Elder tree. She
said it was her
key
    and she walked in the thin radiance of
    a gold beater of stemwear
    and fresh Mosels.
But she was the girl I hated.
And I locked her up in the barn with the imaginary wild
horses.
Tap.
That is a branch scratching the windowpane,
a little wind out there
rocking the trees. My mother
looks in the window.
I know she is three thousand miles away
and I have imagined her face
out there.
Tap.
She rubs her fingers against the glass
and a moth flies off the ceiling. It would like to be
covered
with blood.
I feel that in bed I cannot stir
for the horrors around me: I forget that somewhere
there is you,

a man I love. My memory deserts me or locks you in a tool
shed, somewhere inaccessible,
somewhere beyond the sound of my voice.
My mother tries to visit me in the dead night
and her voice, her face,
are the trees I am so afraid to walk/ among

The White Rabbit
KAREN SWENSON

Yes, Mother,
holding the banister with five-year-old fingers
muffled in Sunday gloves
I did come down the stairs
in my daffodil coat from Best's
in my straw hat with the brown ribbons down my back
and the round elastic that sliced my throat.

Thirty-five years I've tried to remember
what we fought about in your upstairs bedroom
that I've wiped from the inside of my mind —
the house ends for me at the top of the stair —
although I can smell your scent
the bottle with the perched crystal doves.

Dressed in your will of clothes
I watch you pin hat to hair in the mirror
while my small voice hurls itself against you
and a fly blunders into your glass hat
falling into the powder in the pink box.

Like butter on pancakes
the sun melts on the front porch.
I unlatch the hutch
peel the white cotton from my hands
and beat the rabbit to death,
that plump passivity of flesh
soft as your talcumed thighs.

When you discovered the rabbit
your hand snaked the dog chain round my legs
each blow winding and unwinding pain
on the bobbin of my scream.
You beat the badness from your doll.
I wished you dead.

But I kept my secret even while
I carried the cigar box
to your chant of accusations.
All those words have dissolved
into the swamp gas of nightmares.

Twenty years later
you apologized in the car,
said it couldn't have been just me,
must have been all of us
picking it up by the ears—
a hemorrhage.
I listened but didn't confess.
You, eyes taut to the road,
never mentioned the whipping
and I,
now that you're dead
just as I wanted you to be,
come back to climb the stairs.

What If God

SHARON OLDS

And what if God had been watching, when my mother
came into my room, at night, to lie down on me
and pray and cry? What did He do when her
long adult body rolled on me
like lava from the top of the mountain
and the magma popped from her ducts, and my bed
shook from the tremors, the cracking of my nature
across? What was He? Was He a bison
to lower his almost extinct head
and suck his Zeusian phallus while we cried
and prayed to Him, or was He a squirrel
reaching through her hole in my shell, His arm
up to the elbow in the yolk of my soul
stirring, stirring the gold? Or was He
a kid in Biology, dissecting me
while she held my split carapace apart
so He could firk out the eggs, or was He a man
entering me while she pried my spirit
open in the starry dark—
she said that all we did was done in His sight
so He must have been watching and seen her weep
     into my
hair and slip my soul from between my
ribs like a tiny hotel soap, He must have
washed his hands of me as I washed my
hands of Him. Is there a God in the house?
Is there a God in the house? Then reach down
and take that woman off that child's body,
take that woman by the nape of the neck like a young cat
and lift her up, and deliver her over to me.

Mother

ERICA JONG

Ash falls on the roof
of my house.

I have cursed you enough
in the lines of my poems
& between them,
in the silences which fall
like ash flakes
on the water tank
from a smog-bound sky.

I have cursed you
because I remember
the smell of *Joy*
on a sealskin coat
& because I feel
more abandoned than a baby seal
on an ice floe red
with its mother's blood.

I have cursed you
as I walked & prayed
on a concrete terrace
high above the street
because whatever I pulled down
with my bruised hand
from the bruising sky,
whatever lovely plum
came to my mouth

you envied
& spat out.

Because you saw me in your image,
because you favored me,
you punished me.

It was only a form of you
my poems were seeking.
Neither of us knew.

For years
we lived together
in a single skin.

We shared fur coats.
We hated each other
as the soul hates the body
for being weak,
as the mind hates the stomach
for needing food,
as one lover hates the other.

I kicked
in the pouch of your theories
like a baby kangaroo.

I believed you
on Marx, on Darwin,
on Tolstoy & Shaw.
I said I loved Pushkin
(you loved him).

I vowed Monet
was better than Bosch.

Who cared?

I would have said nonsense
to please you
& frequently did.

This took the form,
of course,
of fighting you.

We fought so gorgeously!

We fought like one boxer
& his punching bag.
We fought like mismatched twins.
We fought like the secret sharer
& his shade.

Now we're apart.
Time doesn't heal
the baby to the womb.
Separateness is real
& keeps on growing.

One by one the mothers
drop away,
the lovers leave,
the babies outgrow clothes.

Some get insomnia—
the poet's disease—
& sit up nights
nursing
at the nipples
of their pens.

I have made hot milk
& kissed you where you are.
I have cursed my curses.
I have cleared the air.
& now I sit here writing,
breathing you.

Burn Center

SHARON OLDS

When my mother talks about the Burn Center
she's given to the local hospital
my hair lifts and wavers like smoke
in the air around my head. She speaks of the
beds in her name, the suspension baths and
square miles of lint, and I think of the
years with her, as her child, as if
without skin, walking around scalded
raw, first-degree burns over ninety
percent of my body. I would stick to doorways I
tried to walk through, stick to chairs as I
tried to rise, pieces of my flesh
tearing off easily as
well-done pork, and no one gave me
a strip of gauze, or a pat of butter to
melt on my crackling side, but when I would
cry out she would hold me to her
hot griddle, when my scorched head stank she would
draw me deeper into the burning
room of her life. So when she talks about her
Burn Center, I think of a child
who will come there, float in water
murky as tears, dangle suspended in a
tub of ointment, suck ice while they
put out all the tiny subsidiary
flames in her hair near the brain, and I say,
Let her sleep as long as it takes, let her walk out
without a scar, without a single mark to
honor the power of fire.

Daughterly
KATHLEEN SPIVACK

So many women, writing,
escaped their mothers —
mine, in her nightgown,
retreated into a wordless depression.

If only I could have
spoken for her,
but she turned her face to stone,
her curly hair to snakes,

and her tongue dried up
trying to escape her children.
We skated her surface,
the old ice pond

with its treacherous
depths and greenish patches.
When she melted for moments
she touched my cheek, snowflake,

like a hot penny
burning a hole to my heart.
In her inward chill
I seared myself over,

a young girl
skating away, writing
on air
with a red muffler.

Her silence; my silence:
the house, its stubborn necessities;
the snow, her scabbed
depression, drifted secretly

till even the blades of our
ice skates stopped
their thin persistent scraping on
her winter; the knife-sharp air.

My Mother's Breakfront

JANET STERNBURG

She acquired an eye
for cracks and chips
bargained down the price
the plates were flawed
but hers
and when she turned
the damage to the wall
they looked intact

when I die
these pieces
are for you

Pockets

KAREN SWENSON

The point of clothes was line,
a shallow fall of cotton over childish hips
or a coat ruled sharply, shoulder to hem,

but that line was marred by hands
and all the most amazing things
that traveled in them to one's pockets
goitering the shape of grace with gifts —

a puffball only slightly burst
five links of watch chain passed secretly in class
a scrap of fur almost as soft as one's own skin.

Offended at my pouching of her Singer stitch
my mother sewed my pockets up
with an overcast tight as her mouth
forbidding all but the line.

I've lived for years in her seams —
falls of fabric smooth as slide rules
my hands exposed and folded from all gifts.

And it is only recently, with raw fingers
which still recall the warmth and texture of presents,
that I've plucked out stitches sharp as urchin spines
to find both hands and pockets empty.

My Mother and the Bed
LYN LIFSHIN

no not that way she'd
say when I was 7 pulling
the bottom sheet smooth
you've got to   saying
hospital corners

I wet the bed much later
than I should, until
just writing this I
hadn't thought of
the connection

My mother would never
sleep on sheets someone
else had   I never
saw any stains on hers
tho her bedroom was

a maze of powder   hair
pins   black dresses
Sometimes she brings her
own sheets to my house
carries toilet seat covers

Lyn did anybody sleep
in my she always asks
Her sheets her hair
smell of smoke she
says the rooms here
smell funny

we drive at 3 AM
slow into Boston and
strip what looks like
two clean beds as the
sky gets light   I

smooth on the form-
fitted flower bottom
she redoes it

She thinks of my life
as a bed only she
can make right.

First Menstruation

ELLEN BASS

I had been waiting
waiting for what felt like lifetimes.
When the first girls stayed out of the ocean
a few days a month, wore shorts instead of a swimsuit
I watched them enviously.
I even stayed out once in a while, pretending.

At last, finding blood on my panties
I carried them to my mother, hoping,
unsure, afraid—Mom, is this it?

She gave me Kotex and belt
showed me how to wear it.
Dot Lutz was there, smiling, saying when her Bonnie
got her period, she told her,
When you have questions, come to me, ask me.
You can ask a mother anything.

I felt so strange when she said that.
Mom didn't say anything.

The three of us
standing in the bedroom
me, the woman-child, standing with the older women
and the feeling
there once was a feeling
that should be here,
there once was a rite, a communion.

I said, Yes, I'll ask my mother
but we all, except maybe Dot,
knew it wasn't true.

The Fish
LILA ZEIGER

I had about as much chance, Mother,
as the carp who thrashed
in your bathtub on Friday,
swimming helplessly back and forth
in the small hard pool you made for me,
unaware how soon you would
pull me from my element
sever my head just below the gills
scrape away the iridescence
chop me into bits and pieces and
reshape me with your strong hands
to simmer in your special broth.
You bustled about the house
confident in your design,
while I waited at the edge
imploring you with glossy eyes
to keep me and love me
just as I was.

Meeting in Nérac
COLETTE INEZ

My mother's face, a lantern at the window,
lights a path to her door, to openings I hear
in her voice asking me to climb the stairs
to her book-lined rooms.

I try to read the small print of her lips.
She turns away like a page too quickly skimmed.
The parchment of her skin whispers a story
of two scholars humbled by illicit love,
my lettered sires who signed me away.

When she crosses slowly to the room's far end
and perches on a brown wing chair, she is a queen
in ravelled sleeves who offers me a Baedeker
and the history of her town.
What she won't say floods the room with images:

she is naked, heavy breasts graze the water
as she wades into the river. In a shadowy cove,
the body swims languorously, one arm, then another
pulling her forward to the far shore.
There my father writes marginal notes on the edges
of a manuscript. He will comb her wet hair.
She will hum a song.

"How long is your holiday?" I am pulled short
from my musings by her voice. "The region is filled
with interesting ruins." Her English accent rings
in counterpoint with the sigh of palms on her red-
tiled roof, in the south of France,

where we speak after an absence of long years.
"Next year Halley's comet returns," I say.
She recalls its glow and how she tugged at her father's
arm alongside the same blue-shuttered house
in which we talk of traveling
through the mother country.

Ruler of wanderers and lanterns of night, let her study
the comet one more time. I ask this for a woman of Nérac
from whom I inherit a love of quandaries: my doubt
of heaven, hers of the here and now. What else we meant
to call into question or deny stays unresolved
like an unfocused star.

The Survivors
JUDITH HEMSCHEMEYER

Night after night
She dreamed we were drowned
Or covered with spiders
Or butchered or tortured

She took us all to bed with her

And woke up whimpering
And came to find our bodies
In the dark, brushing our foreheads
Sorting out our tangled limbs

Amazed to find us whole

By day her love for us
Was a prairie fire
That roared across our whole horizon
Burning us out of our burrows

"I touched the windowpane"
"I touched myself"
"I let the boys touch me"

Like small, crazed animals
We leaped before her
Knowing there was no escape

She had to consume us utterly
Over and over again
And now at last
We are her angels
Burned so crisp
We crumble when we try to touch

I Must Have Learned This Somewhere
MOLLY PEACOCK

I loved an old doll made of bleached
wooden beads strung into a stick figure.
When the string was pulled, the tautened limbs
reached their full extent, and a human figure,
stiff with rigor mortis, rose up.
When the string was let go, the doll collapsed
into a heap more lifelike, though it missed
its spinal cord of string. I spent hours trying
to prop it up to look more human without
pulling the string, but it sat in my hands,
bent, uncontrolled in a muscular fit
or a spasm of fear. And so for myself,
collapsed in a tangled necklace,
anger painting my stiff wooden face.
Yet now my life can hold me in its hands
as long ago I coaxed the doll in my palms
to try to sit lifelike there. My mother's hands
must long ago have offered the same balm,
though I took her for an operator
holding my string. How else could I store
such an idea of comfort as I
gave the doll, so material was its cry?

Fifteen to Eighteen
MARILYN HACKER

I'd almost know, the nights I snuck in late,
at two, at three, as soon as I had tucked
into myself tucked in, to masturbate
and make happen what hadn't when I fucked,
there'd be the gargled cry, always "God damn
you to hell," to start with, from the other
bedroom: she was in shock again. I swam
to my surface to take care of my mother.
That meant, run for a glass of orange juice,
clamp her shoulders with one arm, try to pour
it down her throat while she screamed, "No, God damn
you!" She is stronger than I am
when this happens. If she rolls off on the floor,
I can't / she won't let me / lift her up. Fructose
solution, a shot and she'd come around.
At half past two, what doctor could I call?
Sometimes I had to call the hospital.
More often, enough orange juice got down,
splashed on us both.
                                  "What are you doing here?
Where were you? Why is my bed in this mess?
How did you get those scratches on your face?
What were you doing, out until this hour?"

Premonition
(in a voice my mother called "not your own")
YVONNE

It was Mama who was partial
to Aunt Viney, my father's sister.
It was Mama who first said,
What about Jade?
when Aunt Viney had to go back
to the Byberry State Hospital.
It was the fourth time in half a dozen years.
It was Mama who said Uncle Harold
belonged there himself
because all his people was peculiar
especially his mother who was Sanctified
and didn't eat pork or nothing
and didn't believe in doctors or anything
just like my father's mother (and most of his people)
and such a house
couldn't be no good for the child.
So it was Mama
who first took pity
and not Dad.

If Mama came back from Mass
and found Aunt Viney
(who was on some kind of a probation
and living again with her peculiar husband)
and signified she could stay for lunch,
my father would get up from the radio,
leave the house without saying
more than hello

and not come back till past my bedtime.
Then he would have to warm up his own
dinner and get dressed
for the eleven o'clock shift.

But then Aunt Viney
had some kind of a relapse
and Mama went to get little Jade
out of that house
of old folks, Sanctified, and looking
like slaves. Making even that child
look old.
Mama dressed her up in my old clothes
which wasn't raggedy or anything
(Mama being so hard on me)
and we wasn't getting any help
from the court then.
And Mama coated her face with Noxzema,
to get rid of the ash.
And Mama combed and brushed her hair
as much as three times a day
because it needed
a lot of training.

But then we started getting help from the court,
and my father's brothers and sisters
started coming around.
They started getting very tight.
And Mama signified nasty about it.
But when they were gone, my father said,
Don't push me, Evangeline.
Don't push.

Everybody knows Viney is the biggest fool
always crying, always crying and going off—
colored people got better things to do!
A grown colored woman making herself
crazy over the dead—plenty people die!
What she think she is—white?
What she got to be screaming for?
Mama is dead. Period.
And isn't she dead counting on God?

And Mama only said
that Aunt Viney was too young to be
so Sanctified
and she wasn't even
a bad-looking girl, at that.

The Contest of Nerves
PATRICIA TRAXLER

Ma & I were at Louise's house
across the street again

I am so nervous these days Louise
Oh not as bad as me Girl

Ma & Louise
held their hands out
in front of them
over the rusty sink
to see who shook the most

Ma watched Louise's hands
Louise studied Ma's

I watched the shaking of each
accelerate

See Louise
mine are worse
No mine just look Eileen

By this time Louise
was motor powered
but Ma was revving up
and both were frowning now

I announced it was a draw
I was only five but knew some things

The shaking stopped
The subject changed

We had such fun in those days

In the Ocean
PATRICIA GOEDICKE

At first my mother would be shy
Leaving my lame father behind

But then she would tuck up her bathing cap
And fly into the water like a dolphin,

Slippery as bamboo she would bend
Everywhere, everywhere I remember

For though he was always criticizing her,
Blaming her, finding fault

Behind her back he would sneer at her
All through our childhood, to me and my sister,

She never spoke against him

Except to take us by the hand
In the ocean we would laugh together

As we never did, on land

Because he was an invalid
Usually she was silent

But this once, on her deathbed

Hearing me tell it she remembered
Almost before I did, and she smiled

One last time to think of it:
How, with the waves crashing at our feet

Having thrown ourselves upon her, for dear life
Bubbling and splashing for breath,

Slithering all over her wet skin

We would rub against her like minnows
We would flow between her legs, in the surf

Smooth as spaghetti she would hold us
Close against her like small polliwogs climbing

All over her as if she were a hill,
A hill that moved, our element

But hers also, safe
In the oval of each other's arms

This once she would be weightless
As guiltless, utterly free

Of all but what she loved
Smoothly, with no hard edges

My long beautiful mother
In her white bathing cap, crowned

Like an enormous lily

Over the brown arrow of her body
The limber poles of her legs,

The sad slanted eyes,
The strong cheekbones, and the shadows

Like fluid lavender, everywhere

Looping and sliding through the waves
We would swim together as one

In a rainbow of breaking foam

Mother and sea calves gliding,
Floating as if all three of us were flying.

Christmas Eve: My Mother Dressing
TOI DERRICOTTE

My mother was not impressed with her beauty;
once a year she put it on like a costume,
plaited her black hair, slick as corn silk, down past her
    hips,
in one rope-thick braid, turned it, carefully, hand over
    hand,
and fixed it at the nape of her neck, stiff and elegant as a
    crown,
with tortoise pins, like huge insects,
some belonging to her dead mother,
some to my living grandmother.
Sitting on the stool at the mirror,
she applied a peachy foundation that seemed to hold her
    down, to trap her,
as if we never would have noticed what flew among us
    unless it was weighted and bound in its mask.
Vaseline shined her eyebrows,
mascara darkened her lashes until they swept down like
    feathers;
her eyes deepened until they shone from far away.

Now I remember her hands, her poor hands, which, even
    then, were old from scrubbing,
whiter on the inside than they should have been,
and hard, the first joints of her fingers, little fattened pads,
the nails filed to sharp points like old-fashioned ink pens,
    painted a jolly color.

Her hands stood next to her face and wanted to be put
    away, prayed
for the scrub bucket and brush to make them useful.
And, as I write, I forget the years I watched her
pull hairs like a witch from her chin, magnify
every blotch — as if acid were thrown from the inside.

But once a year my mother
rose in her white silk slip,
not the slave of the house, the woman,
took the ironed dress from the hanger —
allowing me to stand on the bed, so that
my face looked directly into her face,
and hold the garment away from her
as she pulled it down.

White Gloves
MARY MAKOFSKE

In the dim room sour-sweet
with fever, my mother
ladled ice cream
on my burning tongue.
Outside, day melted into
night, and no tomorrow
could scar me enough
to keep my nails from clawing
the pox erupting on my skin.

My mother brought me
her good white gloves,
worked them gently down
around my fingers,
saying, *Now you are a lady.*
And I was, lifting my hands
in the darkness, their white gleam
a shield between my urges
and my nettlesome body.

Pale sheath of *lady*,
how you melted
against those later fevers,
the itch of desire.
My mother dangled her white gloves
before me, but I saw her wearing
her flesh with ease,
the beautiful breasts,

the curves of her feet
barely contained
in her summer sandals.

My Mother Was Always Dressed
ABIGAIL THOMAS

She wore lipstick and powder
and her face smelled good.
one winter she wore a bearskin coat
and a purple hat from Guatemala
with a tassel.

the summer she wore a bathing suit
she stood me in front of her
and was photographed.
I look at us, squinting into the sun,
her body hidden behind mine.

once, in the gloom of the bathhouse,
I peeked at her naked.
her nipples were dark and alien,
and she smelled like soup.

Touching/Not Touching: My Mother
TOI DERRICOTTE

1.
That first night in the hotel bedroom,
when the lights go out,
she is already sleeping (that woman who has always
claimed sleeplessness), inside her quiet breathing
like a long red gown. How can she
sleep? My heart beats as if I am alone,
for the first time, with a lover or a beast.
Will I hate her drooping mouth,
her old-woman rattle? Once I nearly
suffocated on her breast. Now I can almost
touch the other side of my life.

2.
Undressing
in the dark,
looking,
not looking,
we parade before each other,
old proud peacocks, in our stretch marks
with hanging butts. We are equals. No
more do I need to wear her high heels to step
inside the body of a woman.
Her beauty and strangeness no longer seduce
me out of myself. I show my good side, my
long back, strong mean legs, my thinness that
came from learning to hold back
from taking what's not mine. No more
a thief for love. She takes off her

bra, facing me, and I see those gorgeous
globes, soft, creamy,
high; my mouth waters.
How will I resist
crawling in beside her, putting
my hand for warmth
under her thin nightdress?

When the Skins Fall Apart

DARA WIER

The fertilizer plant grinds fish into stink.
In the icebox a dove carcass cools while Moma
boils pumpkin in a castiron pot.

The house upfront is full of drying garlic
where you wait for the boy from Buras.
Riversand's soft as any barnbed.

You two roll in the garlic bulbs shaking the skin to pieces.
Moma stuffs shirts in starch clabber, twists them
into clubs and puts them aside for ironing.

After the first time you go home, helping
Moma fix supper. You wonder why this takes so long.
On your stomach the white scale of dried sperm,

you spit on it to get the smell. Moma presses
blouses, white dress shirts, the starch drying
under her nails.

You take a razor to cut the blister
school shoes give your heels, pitching
the skin in the river.

When the cold lasts too long, too hard, green
oranges rot on the limbs. The knot on your belly
turns in like a knot on a navel orange.

You wish your stomach would drop off.
You dice up garlic heads, their smell
like drying blood lasts all day on your hands.

Burns

SANDRA HOBEN

The cat brushes past
and the shade of the bronze lamp
leans against the bulb —
another brown flower
blossoms on the pale cloth.
I made this shade myself,
stitching the big, vague roses
of a cotton shirt onto a cone
of wire. Now smell it —
the laundry room, twenty years ago,
my mother staring
at the clouded window, the iron
sinking into linen, leaving
a black ship
that won't push off again.

1973

MARILYN HACKER

"I'm pregnant," I wrote to her in delight
from London, thirty, married, in print. A fools-
cap sheet scrawled slantwise with one minuscule
sentence came back. "I hope your child is white."
I couldn't tear the pieces small enough.
I hoped she'd be black as the ace of spades,
though hybrid beige heredity had made
that as unlikely as the spun-gold stuff
sprouted after her neonatal fur.
I grudgingly acknowledged her "good hair,"
which wasn't, very, from my point of view.
"No tar brush left," her father's mother said.
"She's Jewish and she's white," from her cranked bed
mine smugly snapped.
                                    She's Black. She is a Jew.

The Dirty-Billed Freeze Footy
JUDITH HEMSCHEMEYER

Remember that Saturday morning
Mother forgot the word gull?

We were all awake but still in bed
and she called out, "Hey kids!

What's the name of that bird that eats garbage
and stands around in cold water on the beach?"

And you, the quick one, the youngest daughter,
piped right back: "A dirty-billed freeze footy!"

And she laughed till she was weak,
until it hurt her. And you had done it:

reduced our queen to warm and helpless rubble.

And the rest of the day, baking or cleaning
or washing our hair until it squeaked,

whenever she caught sight of you
it would start all over again.

My Mother and the Matches
LYN LIFSHIN

She said I didn't know you
couldn't either   my mother
who knew which man was
circumcised and which
woman's laugh I like

light matches? no we both
laugh we couldn't and
nearly flunked chemistry
One day when my lab partner
didn't come the Bunsen
burner stayed unlit

At Raven's I cripple four
cardboard-boxed matches and
can't admit I'm afraid
to be burnt

a whole year dreaming of
fires, my mother up all night
other Aprils sniffing
for smoke. My

mother had once said you
mean you'd swallow it but
she never   until this
morning talked about
her fear of matches

startling   as knowing she
has a down quilt from
Russia in a closet
I've never seen   I

tell her I never lit a candle
till the lights went out that
fall for two days and then

I lit it on the electric
stove   never cooked tea
in a house with a
gas stove

Blue cabin in Maine
with just the wood stove
that had to be kept burning
I hardly slept 3 days

and do you hate to kill flies my
mother asks like Columbus
discovering a new continent

Color of Honey
ANNE WALDMAN

mother's got salve
mother's got a way to go
mother's a sacristy
mother keep the germs away
protect us, mother
your little angel with cunt wings
mother, a big brain
mother, smarter than the little girl
mother, I must complete my solo
mother, I rebuff you
mother, I adore you
you're my true lover never fear
mother, I know I scowl I
don't mean to
see the starkness of morning, mother!
smell the sweet alyssum
here's my comely man to meet you
here's my lovely lady to see you
mother, the clams are all female
here's my saline self to mix with you
we're autochthonous
we're gathering wool
we're weaving a garment
we're very sophisticated
we don't need a try-out
we're combing the beach now
we're fixed stars we're binary stars
you're standing over me
you're standing behind me

you're standing by me
you're at my feet
you be my moon you be my
tormentor you howl at me
you lock me in my room
you keep me wise
you be my milk you be
my book, my tigress,
my sparrow hawk, my steed
you correcting me
with your soft eyes
bright lipstick in a brown suit
color of honey

summer words of a sistuh addict
SONIA SANCHEZ

the first day i shot dope
was on a sunday.
    i had just come
home from church
     got mad at my motha
cuz she got mad at me. u dig?
      went out. shot up
behind a feelen gainst her.
      it felt good.
gooder than dooing it. yeah.
       it was nice.
i did it. uh. huh. i did it. uh. huh.
i want to do it again. it felt so gooooood.
   and as the sistuh
   sits in her silent/
   remembered/high
   someone leans for
   ward gently asks her:
     sistuh.
     did u
     finally
   learn how to hold yo/mother?
and the music of the day
     drifts in the room
to mingle with the sistuh's young tears.
   and we all sing.

Mothers

NIKKI GIOVANNI

the last time i was home
to see my mother we kissed
exchanged pleasantries
and unpleasantries pulled a warm
comforting silence around
us and read separate books

i remember the first time
i consciously saw her
we were living in a three-room
apartment on burns avenue

mommy always sat in the dark
i don't know how i knew that but she did

that night i stumbled into the kitchen
maybe because i've always been
a night person or perhaps because i had wet
the bed
she was sitting on a chair
the room was bathed in moonlight diffused through
those thousands of panes landlords who rented
to people with children were prone to put in windows

she may have been smoking but maybe not
her hair was three quarters her height
which made me a strong believer in the samson myth
and very black

i'm sure i just hung there by the door
i remember thinking: what a beautiful lady

she was very deliberately waiting
perhaps for my father to come home
from his night job or maybe for a dream
that had promised to come by
"come here" she said "i'll teach you
a poem: *i see the moon*
       the moon sees me
       god bless the moon
       and god bless me"
i taught it to my son
who recited it for her
just to say we must learn
to bear the pleasures
as we have borne the pains

Poem for My Mother
SIV CEDERING

Remember when I draped
the ruffled cotton cape
around your shoulders,
turned off the lights
and stood behind your chair,
brushing, brushing your hair.

The friction of the brush
in the dry air
of that small inland town
created stars that flew
as if God himself was there
in the small space
between my hand and your hair.

Now we live on separate coasts
of a foreign country.
A continent stretches between us.
You write of your illness,
your fear of blindness.
You say you wake afraid
to open your eyes.

Mother, if some morning
you open your eyes to see
daylight as a dark room around you,
I will drape a ruffled cotton cape
around your shoulders
and stand behind your chair,
brushing the stars out of your hair.

Dear Mama (4)
WANDA COLEMAN

when did we become friends?
it happened so gradual i didn't notice
maybe i had to get my run out first
take a big bite of the honky world and choke on it
maybe that's what has to happen with some uppity
    youngsters
if it happens at all

and now
the thought stark and irrevocable
of being here without you
shakes me

beyond love, fear, regret or anger
into that realm children go
who want to care for/protect their parents
as if they could
and sometimes the lucky ones do

into the realm of making every moment
important
laughing as though laughter wards off death
each word given
received like spanish eight

treasure to bury within
against that shadow day
when it will be the only coin i possess
with which to buy peace of mind

Little Red Riding Hood
OLGA BROUMAS

I grow old, old
without you, Mother, landscape
of my heart. No child, no daughter between my bones
has moved and passed
out screaming, dressed in her mantle of blood,

as I did
once through your pelvic scaffold, stretching it
like a wishbone, your tenderest skin
strung on its bow and tightened
against the pain. I slipped out like an arrow, but not before

the midwife
plunged to her wrist and guided
my baffled head to its first mark. High forceps
might, in that one instant, have accomplished
what you and that good woman failed
in all these years to do: cramp
me between the temples, hobble
my baby feet. Dressed in my red hood, howling, I went—

evading
the white-clad doctor and his fancy claims: microscope,
stethoscope, scalpel, all
the better to see with, to hear,
and to eat—straight from your hollowed basket
into the midwife's skirts. I grew up

good at evading, and when you said,
"Stick to the road and forget the flowers, there's
wolves in those bushes, mind
where you got to, mind
you get there," I
minded. I kept

to the road, kept
the hood secret, kept what it sheathed more
secret still. I opened
it only at night, and with other women
who might be walking the same road to their own
grandmas' house, each with her basket of gifts, her small
    hood
safe in the same part. I minded well. I have no daughter

to trace that road back to your lap with my laden
basket of love. I'm growing
old, old
without you. Mother, landscape
of my heart, architect of my body, what other gesture
can I conceive

to make with it
that would reach you, alone
in your house and waiting, across this improbable forest
peopled with wolves and our lost, flower-gathering
sisters they feed on.

Heredity

HEATHER MCHUGH

My mother grows emaciated
in the Danish modern chair.

I have fattened past the dotted
limits of my assigned space, my cells,

my DNA, and forget I was ever afraid
to speak. My mother cannot finish

a sentence. I know how to unwind
her helices of tears. I know

which hairpin keeps her
from going haywire, know how far

I'd have to walk to put
unwooden arms around her, hug her

till the struts shook. When will I see
you again, she wonders, adjusting

her glasses. Don't mention
your father. Marry the man

of my dreams. Wear my bathrobe
with its yellow leashes. Let me

love you, need you,
know you, let me

go. The things we cannot say
slip buttered knives through the venetian blinds.

She cleans her glasses, says beneath
her breath the town is not the same. My tongue

goes over and over
its old home ground, in which, today, were fixed

these two new slick
white stones, my own

false teeth.

A Daughter (1)

DENISE LEVERTOV

When she was in the stranger's house—
good strangers, almost relatives, good house,
so familiar, known for twenty years,
its every sound at once, and without thought,
interpreted:
        but alien, deeply alien—
when she was there last week, part of her wanted
only to leave. It said *I must escape*—no,
crudely in the vernacular: *I gotta get outta here*,
it said.

And part of her
ached for her mother's pain,
her dying here—at home, yet far away from home,
thousands of miles of earth and sea and ninety years
from her roots. The daughter's one happiness
during the brief visit that might be her last
(no, last but one: of course there could always be
what had stood for years at the end of some highway of
factual knowledge, a terminal wall;
there would be words to deal with; funeral, burial, disposal
    of effects;
the books to pack up)—her one happiness this time
was to water her mother's treasured, fenced-in garden,
a Welsh oasis where she remembers adobe rubble
two decades ago. Will her mother now
ever rise from bed, walk out of her room,
                  see if her yellow rose
has bloomed again?

Rainbows, the dark earthfragrance, the whisper of arched
    spray
the pleasure goes back
to the London garden, forty, fifty years ago,
her mother, younger than she is now.
And back in the north, watering the blue ajuga
                    (far from beginnings too; but it's a place
                    she's chosen as home)
the daughter knows
another, hidden, part of her longed — or longs —
for her mother to be her mother again,
consoling, judging, forgiving,
whose arms were once
                    strong to hold her and rock her, . . .

Present

TESS GALLAGHER

She could hold me with stories, even
those about people whose names and doings
were feathers, a fluttering at
the brain, scattered or wafted in the current
of her voice, softly away. Those lives
happened out of her and into me and out
again, because I couldn't remember, only be
warmed by them. Somehow my forgetting insured
returns to that hovering population in her
memory, of which, as I found, I was a part.

She said she thought maybe she couldn't have
children, maybe nothing would come. She
and my father together by then two years.
His being dead now, not coming into this, but
there too, as if he couldn't hear us,
but we could know for him. "I'd go up into
the woods where he was logging, do what I could,
work hard as two men myself. That day

on Round Mountain your dad and his partner
got ahead of me. I'd been working.
I hadn't seen where I was. Suddenly I was
alone, walking this old logging road, fireweed
over my head. I stood still and listened
to the birds and other sounds — wind and
little fallings and shiftings in the undergrowth,
animal stirrings. It's so beautiful

here! I kept thinking. I've never been anywhere
so beautiful! I was alone with the mountain. Sun

shattering down through the trees onto ferns
and fallen logs. It's peaceful here, I thought.
Then it came to me, like the mountain had told
me, and I knew it was over. One waiting was
over. And another was starting. The feeling so
sure I put my hands on my belly and pressed
a little against where the carrying had started
before I'd known it. Knowing then, so you'd
stopped happening without me. 'We,' I thought,
'We.' And I thought of your father not

knowing yet, and it seemed you were knowing for
him already, were rushing ahead of me like
an action I had no part in, but was all of me
and some of him that I was about to let you tell
him. Isn't that what conception is? Agreeing
to take the consequences of things so far
beyond you that a trembling takes over and more
is shaken out of us than we can
possible account for?" And something else, she
said, the elevation of mountains, the way

beauty makes things want to join
each other. Then far off, like an echo of
itself, the *swish-swish* of the crosscut,
the steady rhythm of the blade limber against
a tree. She started to walk, still thinking how
beautiful it was all around her, the partnership

of the saw blade raking through the silence
as she made her way toward the faraway
splintering, the rending of the heartwood she
knew would fall, would crash down, shuddering

the length of itself against the trees still
standing, while like a deer, picking its way
through underbrush to the edge of
the clearing, she moved, until
they saw her back into human shape. A woman
whose whereabouts they had wondered vaguely
about as they worked. And as she joined them,
they kept on with their working.

Seasons of the War
For foster mother, Ruth

COLETTE INEZ

In the foggy spring of the far-off war,
what could I have given her?
A wind-up doll instead of the child
the doctor told her might cure pinched
nerves, migraines, a fraying marriage of
fifteen years. What did she want?

I wanted her amber pomade, lip balm,
lotions, and lilac cologne, little jars of
rouge, vanishing creams, the lie of
"You are beautiful."

In the summer of the war,
on our porch with the blue glider
and white wicker chairs, what did she want?
Another start? Another drink? A body
not tricking her with blissful dreams
of mothering?

I longed to step into her paisley dress
with the fringed epaulets, to button
her yellow silk blouse, black birds on it.
I wanted them to fly out of her small breasts,
to sing to us in the morning.

In the stormy fall of the year,
I found her naked body in the hall.
"One too many," someone said. I'd seen the shot

glasses lined up on the bar downstairs
where she sat on a stool that spun
like a record on a phonograph.

Rumba tunes pulsed softly
when she convalesced. In her peach robe
and matching bandeau pulling back her hair,
how fragile she was and inconsolable.

I envied her cream of tomato soup,
orange pekoe tea, the red lacquered tray
with parasols stenciled in gold.
They were close to her.

"What can I do?" I wanted to run to the store for her.
"Go comb your hair," I was dismissed.
She'd return to exposés in *True Confessions*,
Silver Screen.

I stole her tortoiseshell mirror,
her apple green comb
in the winter when F.D.R. declared war here.
She huddled by the radio,
sipping double scotches, straight.
"My nerves are raw," she'd sigh
and drape a hand across her eyes.
I learned to tiptoe up the stairs.

The war streaked headlines, dark bands
of birds, flying in a line.
Spring came. Summer. One day
she didn't answer to her name.

I thought I could have caught her last breath
in the tortoiseshell mirror,
parted her hair with the apple green comb.

She was laid out in a beige
lace gown, lavender sash, her face
a peaceful mask, but I stood by the casket
in a pink, puffed dress and choked back rage
as if it were a bone stuck in my throat.

Later, alone in her room, I did a rumba
with her empty clothes, held on to the sleeves,
imagined her soul lolling on the deck

of a Caribbean party boat.
And I combed and combed my hair.

My Mother Remembers That She Was Beautiful
for Georgia Morris Bond

TESS GALLAGHER

The falling snow has made her thoughtful
and young in the privacy
of our table with its netted candle
and thick white plates. The serious faces
of the lights breathe on the pine boards
behind her. She is visiting
the daughter never close
or far enough away to come to.

She keeps her coat on, called into
her girlhood by such forgetting
I am gone or yet
to happen. She sees herself
among the townspeople, the country glances
slow with fields and sky
as she passes or waits
with a brother in the hot animal smell
of the auction stand: sunlight,
straw hats, a dog's tail
brushing her bare leg.

"There are things you know.
I didn't have to beg," she said, "for anything."

The beautiful one speaks to me
from the changed, proud face and I see
how little I've let her know
of what she becomes. Years

were never the trouble, or the white hair
I braided near the sea
on a summer day. Who
she must have been
is lost to me through some fault
in my own reflection and we will have to go on
as we think we are, walking for no one's sake
from the empty restaurant into the one color
of the snow — before us, the close houses,
the brave and wondering lights of the houses.

from Mourning Pictures

HONOR MOORE

Ladies and gentlemen, my mother is
dying. You say, "Everyone's mother dies."
I bow to you, smile. Ladies, gentlemen,
my mother is dying. She has cancer.
You say "Many people die of cancer."
I scratch my head. Gentle ladies, gentle
men, my mother has cancer, and, short of
some miracle, will die. You say "This has
happened many times before." You say "Death
is something which repeats itself." I bow.
Ladies and gentlemen, my mother has cancer
all through her. She will die unless there's a
miracle. You shrug. You gave up religion
years ago. Marxism too. You don't believe
in **anyth**ing. I step forward. My mother
is dying. I don't believe in miracles.
Ladies and gentlemen, one last time: My
mother's dying. I haven't got another.

What Remains
MARGE PIERCY

These ashes are not the fine dust I imagined.
The undertaker brings them out from the back
in a plastic baggie, like supermarket produce.
I try not to grab, but my need shocks me,
how I hunger to seize this officially
labeled garbage and carry you off.

All the water was vaporized,
the tears, the blood, the sweat,
fluids of a juicy, steamy woman,
burnt offering into the humid Florida
air among cement palm trees with brown
fronds stuck up top like feather dusters.

In the wind the palmettos clatter.
The air is yellowed with dust.
I carry you back North where you belong
through the bumpy black December night
on the almost empty plane stopping
at every airport like a dog at posts.

Now I hold what is left in my hands:
bone bits, segments of the arched skull
varicolored stones of the body,
green, copper, beige, black, purple
fragments of shells eroded by storm
that slowly color the beach.

Archaeology in a plastic baggie.
Grit spills into my palms:

reconstruct your days, your odyssey.
These are fragments of a smashed mosaic
that formed the face of a dancer
with bound feet, cursing in dreams.

At the marriage of the cat and dog
I howl under the floor.
You will chew on each other's bones
for years. You cannot read
the other's body language.
On the same diet you starve.

My longest, oldest love, I have brought
you home to the land I am dug into.
I promise a path laid right to you,
roses to spring from you, herbs nearby,
the company of my dead cats
whose language you already know.

We'll make your grave by piney woods,
a fine place to sit and sip wine,
to take the sun and watch the beans
grow, the tomatoes swell and redden.
You will smell rosemary, thyme,
and the small birds will come.

I promise to hold you in the mind
as a cupped hand protects a flame.
That is nothing to you. You cannot
hear. Yet just as I knew when you
really died, you know I have brought
you home. Now you want to be roses.

A Woman Mourned by Daughters

ADRIENNE RICH

Now, not a tear begun,
we sit here in your kitchen,
spent, you see, already.
You are swollen till you strain
this house and the whole sky.
You, whom we so often
succeeded in ignoring!
You are puffed up in death
like a corpse pulled from the sea;
we groan beneath your weight.
And yet you were a leaf,
a straw blown on the bed,
you had long since become
crisp as a dead insect.
What is it, if not you,
that settles on us now
like satin you pulled down
over our bridal heads?
What rises in our throats
like food you prodded in?
Nothing could be enough.
You breathe upon us now
through solid assertions
of yourself: teaspoons, goblets,
seas of carpet, a forest
of old plants to be watered,
an old man in an adjoining
room to be touched and fed.
And all this universe

dares us to lay a finger
anywhere, save exactly
as you would wish it done.

Wreck Diving
MEG FILES

In her swimming pool, she
is gone. I am here
beneath the rife maples
of my childhood. Grackles

drop onto the lawn: I see
the glossy black bodies and the heads,
oily dark blue, like the ravens
in a Japanese shrine settling down

among the wooden prayers
clacking on the bushes.
I sink face up below summer.
Those above are coasting

on rafts, sipping mai tais
and weeping. From below, I see
the pocked skin of rain
on the sea. Also surviving

are two daughters who hear
the grackles above the fence
and one who settles
into the lucid blue, to the perfect

wreck of her house, all her pictures
so, preserved in salt, the lists,
the laundry, the letters prepared.
I am hungry and nauseous, and the only

answer is she with ginger ale and crackers.
This pool has become the sea —
lucid, pocked, grackle-cried,
and salted from above,

from below. Surviving in the pungent
world are three daughters
and the mother, salt and prayers
ascending through the liquid life.

The Annuity
MARGE PIERCY

1.
When I was fifteen we moved
from a tight asbestos shoe box
to a loose drafty two-story house,
my own tiny room prized under the eaves.
My privacy formed like a bud from the wood.

In my pale green womb I scribbled,
evolving from worm to feral cat,
gobbling books, secreting bones,
building a spine one segment
at a time out of Marx and Freud.

Across the hall the roomers lived,
the couple from Appalachia who cooked
bacon in their room. At a picnic
she miscarried. I held her
in foaming blood. Lost twins.

Salesmen, drab, dirty in the bathroom,
solitary, with girly magazines,
detective stories and pads of orders,
invoices, reports that I would inherit
to write my poems on;

overgrown boys dogging you
out to the backyard with the laundry
baskets; middle-aged losers with eyes
that crawled under my clothes
like fleas and made me itch;

those who paid on time and those
with excuses breaking out like pimples
at the end of the month.
I slammed my door and left them,
ants on the dusty plain.

For the next twenty years
you toted laundry down two flights,
cleaned their bathroom every morning,
scrubbed at the butt burns,
sponged up the acid of their complaints,

read their palms and gave common-
sense advice, fielded their girlfriends,
commiserated with their ex-wives,
lied to their creditors, brewed
tisanes and told them to eat fruit.

What did you do with their checks?
Buy yourself dresses, candy, leisure?
You saved, waiting for the next depression.
You salted it away and Father took control,
investing and then spending as he chose.

2.
Months before you died, you had us drive
south to Florida because you insisted
you wanted to give me things I must carry back.
What were they? Some photographs, china
animals my brother had brought home from
World War II, a set of silver plate.

Then the last evening while Father watched
a game show, you began pulling out dollar
bills, saying, *Shush, don't let him
see, don't let him know.* A five-dollar
bill stuffed under the bobby pins,
ten dollars furled in an umbrella,

wads of singles in the bottom of closet
dividers full of clothes. You shoved
them in my hands, into my purse,
you thrust them at Woody and me.
Take, you kept saying, *I want you to have
it, now while I can, take.*

That night in the hotel room
we sat on the floor counting money
as if we had robbed a candy store:
eighteen hundred in nothing larger
than a twenty, squirreled away, saved
I can't stand to imagine how.

That was the gift you had that felt
so immense to you we would need a car
to haul it back, maybe a trailer too,
the labor of your small deceit
that you might give me an inheritance,
that limp wad salvaged from your sweat.

Selling Her Engagement Ring
KAREN SWENSON

You'd have thought her diamond was set in my flesh
it cost me so much to sell it.
They had me look at it through the loupe to see
how the facets had been chipped
by the marriage it foreshadowed.

But I could not wear the purchase of her domestication
for which she bartered small prairie towns,
clutches of clapboard adrift on the green swell of wheat,
shabby hotels which creaked
room to room of harrow and hosiery salesmen,
as she worked out the pitch
for the next Farmers' Association,
selling Chautauqua lectures across the plain.

I push her diamond across
the jeweler's glass counter,
exchange her bribe for an amethyst
to wear on my wedding bone,
to wear on the hand that bears the age spot on the vein
exactly where it was on hers —
her gift to me as sure as the black spot
Blind Pew gave Bill in *Treasure Island.*

My stone lays its bruise
of color on my hand as I smooth
maps across the dining-room table
choosing my route, a punctuation of prairie towns —
Wahpeton — Mandan — Medora — to vanishing point.

Mint Leaves at Yaddo

LYN LIFSHIN

In frosty glasses of
tea. Here, iced
tea is what we
make waiting for

death with this
machine my mother
wanted. Not knowing
if she'd still be

here for her birth-
day we still shopped
madly, bought her
this present for.

For twenty days my
mother shows only
luke warm interest
in tea, vomits even

water, but I unpack
the plastic, intent
on trying this
sleak device while

my mother, queen
of gadgets,
—even a gun to
demolish flies—

maybe the strangest
thing she got me
can still see the
tall glasses that

seem summery on what
is the longest day.
Soon the light
will go she says,

the days get shorter.
I can't bear, she
murmurs, another
winter in Stowe and

I think how different
this isolation is,
this iced tea, this
time that stretches

where little grows
as it did, green
as that mint, except

my mother, smaller,
more distant, gaunt.

Legacies
HONOR MOORE

White envelope addressed to your mother in red ink — your
   hand; my journal reread after five years: *I hope*
      she doesn't die; a Wanda Landowska
    record pulled from a dusty shelf — I play her,
playing as you did, Bach over and over, when I was
   a child; young composer, jazz singer mother ten years
      dead, stands with me in a cellar, smokes,
waits for laundry: "Just before she died," he says, "my mother
   said, if you become a musician, I want you to
      stand someday on a stage, sing this." He turns
    his back, sings, *When there are gray clouds, I don't mind*
the gray clouds, I'm all for you sonny boy, all for you. Mom,
   I miss you and he tells me it doesn't go away.
      Mom, last winter in this room I cried
in a man's arms, my willingness to love stretching to
   reach someone alive: it was as if I could see my
      heart below me, dark, a mountain range watched
    from a cruising jet. I was crying and I saw death
move out of me, swiftly, like the massed shadows of clouds,
   black, seen from the sky on a clear day, recede, leaving
      just sunlight. Mom: your music, her hands, the
keys moving, live, forceful, speaking — the harpsichord —
   prelude,
    fugue, prelude — past death. Mom, after five years I believe
      and can't believe you died. Last night, the wind,
    a window opening: "Mom," I shout, half joke,
"Mom!" remembering the strong strange wind in the huge
   maples
    the night they called to say you'd gone into a coma.

Tomorrow you're fifty-five. Mom, I'm
thirty-two, and the you that lives on in me sometimes
is not enough. Mom, I wear my hair pulled back with combs.
Mom, I keep my room neat, exercise. Mom,
I ride a horse once a week and keep seeing
you take Grandma's bay mare through that course of
jumps: over and
over: I am a child, the horse throws you. In that dusk
I begin to learn what it might be
to lose you, but always you walk back, stride back, embarrassed,
glasses broken, wet from your fall in the evening
grass, no gray in your black hair. Mom, when I
visited your grave in the snow and could not
move from the hillside because in the cold I saw your mouth
pinken to its living color and smile at me, Mom,
was that real? I sit in this room,
orange curtains billowing in the light—flowers, basket,
star stitched through the Amish quilt—magenta, green,
blue—your
colors, and the dead woman plays as if
alive, moving her long hands, making a deep
sinewy river of each delicate baroque line: Mom,
I am thirty-two. The you that lives on in me is
sometimes not enough. You died before
your mother. You can't know what it is not to have one. There's
snow on the ground here as there was in Massachusetts
the day they buried Grandma. Months after
you died, she told this dream: a place with snow, she
thinks Canada. You are dead but alive, and she rocks you,
rocks you, and you forgive her. Mom, does she rock you now
or do you rock her? At the funeral
the priest said, Our sister enters the gates of paradise

in a company of angels. Mom, were you waiting?
     I have no mother, your mother's gone, and
     the you that lives on, me, I must learn she is
enough. From this room I see snow. Snow. Tomorrow is your
birthday. This is for you. The snow is melting. I've built
     a fire. Mom, the fingers of the dead
woman play as if in some paradise, paradise, and
     your mouth pinkens to breathing red and smiles. I am here,
          your daughter, wanting. *When there are gray*
clouds, I don't mind the gray clouds. I'm all for you. All from you.

Duet for One Voice
LINDA PASTAN

1.
I sit at your side
watching the tides of consciousness
move in and out, watching
the nurses, their caps
like so many white gulls circling
the bed. The window
grows slowly dark,
and light again,
and dark. The clock
tells the same old stories.
Last week you said, Now
you'll have to learn
to sew for yourself.
If the thread is boredom,
the needle is grief.
I sit here learning.

2.
In place of spring
I offer this branch
of forsythia
whose yellow blossoms
I have forced.
You force a smile
in thanks. Outside
it is still cold;
who knows how long
the cold will last?

But underground,
their banners still furled,
whole armies of flowers wait.

3.
I am waiting for you to die,
even as I try to coax you
back to life
with custards and soup
and colored pills I shake
from the bottle like dice,
though their magic
went out of the world
with my surgeon father,
the last magician.
I am waiting
for you to be again
what you always were,
for you to be there whole
for me to run to with this new grief —
your death — the hair grown back
on your skull the way it used to be,
your widow's peak the one sure landmark
on the map of my childhood,
those years when I believed
that medicine and love and being good
could save us all.

4.
We escape from our mothers
again and again, young
Houdinis, playing the usual matinees.

First comes escape down
the birth canal, our newly carved faces
leading the way like figureheads
on ancient slave ships,
our small hands rowing for life.
Later escape into silence, escape
behind slammed doors,
the flight into marriage.
I thought I was finally old enough
to sit with you, sharing a book.
But when I look up
from the page, you
have escaped from me.

The Envelope
MAXINE KUMIN

It is true, Martin Heidegger, as you have written,
I fear to cease, even knowing that at the hour
of my death my daughters will absorb me, even
knowing they will carry me about forever
inside them, an arrested fetus, even as I carry
the ghost of my mother under my navel, a nervy
little androgynous person, a miracle
folded in lotus position.

Like those old pear-shaped Russian dolls that open
at the middle to reveal another and another, down
to the pea-sized, irreducible minim,
may we carry our mothers forth in our bellies.
May we, borne onward by our daughters, ride
in the Envelope of Almost-Infinity,
that chain letter good for the next twenty-five
thousand days of their lives.

Contributor Notes

Ellen Bass has published several volumes of poetry, the most recent being *Our Stunning Harvest*, and is coauthor of *The Courage to Heal: A Guide for Women Survivors of Child Sexual Abuse*. She lives in Santa Cruz, California.

Olga Broumas's first book in English, *Beginning with O*, was the Yale Younger Poets selection in 1977. Her other books include *Soie Sauvage*, *Pastoral Jazz*, *Perpetua*, translations of the Greek poet Odysseas Elytis, and *What I Love* and *Little Mariner*, both published with Copper Canyon Press. A recipient of both Guggenheim and National Endowment for the Arts (NEA) fellowships, she is currently translating the essays of Odysseas Elytis with T. Begley. Ms. Broumas is a bodywork therapist in Provincetown, Massachusetts, and teaches at Boston University and Brandeis.

Siv Cedering is the author of fifteen books, chapbooks, and books of translations, including *Oxen*, *Letters from the Floating World*, and *Twelve Pages from the Floating World*. Her poetry has appeared in *Harper's Magazine*, *Ms.*, the *New*

Republic, the *New York Times* and the *Paris Review*. Her stories have appeared in *Partisan Review*, the *Georgia Review*, *Fiction International*, *Shenandoah*, *Confrontation*, and in many anthologies. Ms. Cedering is also a visual artist who has illustrated four books for children and one book of poetry with photographs.

Lucille Clifton has published several volumes of poetry, including *Good Times*, *Good News About the Earth*, *Ten Oxherding Poems*, and *Good Woman: Collected Poems*.

Wanda Coleman, a native of Los Angeles, is a poet, essayist, fiction and script writer who has received fellowships in literature from the Guggenheim Foundation and the NEA. She presently cohosts "The Poetry Connexion," an interview program, with Austin Straus for California's Pacifica radio network. *Heavy Daughter Blues*, her collection of poems and stories from 1968 to 1986, was published by Black Sparrow Press.

Toi Derricotte has published three collections of poetry: *Natural Birth*, *The Empress of the Death House*, and, most recently, *Captivity*, from the University of Pittsburgh Press. She is the recipient of two fellowships from the NEA, as well as grants from the New Jersey State Council on Arts and the Maryland State Arts Council. She has received the Lucille Medwick Memorial Award from the Poetry Society of America, a Pushcart Prize, and the Folger Shakespeare Library Poetry Committee Book Award. Ms. Dericotte is associate professor of English at the University of Pittsburgh and lives in Potomac, Maryland, with her husband.

Diane di Prima was born in Brooklyn, New York, a second-generation American of Italian descent. She lived and wrote in Manhattan for many years, where she became known as the most important woman writer of the Beat movement. During that time she cofounded the New York Poets Theatre and the Poets Press. For the past twenty years she has lived and worked in northern California; she is currently based in San Francisco, where she is one of the cofounders of and teachers at the San Francisco Institute of Magical and Healing Arts. Her current works in progress include *Not Quite Buffalo Stew*, a satire of California life, and *Recollections of My Life as a Woman*, an autobiographical memoir, presently being serialized by *Mama Bear's News and Notes* in Oakland.

Barbara Eve was born in Chicago and now lives in New York. Her poems have appeared in *Esquire*, *Antaeus*, the *Nation*, and the *Agni Review*.

Meg File's poems and stories have appeared in publications such as *Bloomsbury Review*, the *Tampa Review*, and the *Nebraska Review*. Her novel *Meridian 144*, about post-nuclear survival as well as a mother-and-daughter relationship, was published in 1991 by Soho Press.

Kathleen Fraser published and edited *How(ever)* from 1983 to 1989. Her most recent collection of poems is *Notes Preceding Trust* from the Lapis Press, and her chapbook, *Giotta: Arena* was published by Abacus in late 1991. Ms. Fraser lives in Rome for part of each year and teaches in the M.F.A. in Creative Writing program of San Francisco State University.

Tess Gallagher's most recent book of poetry, *Amplitude: New and Selected Poems*, was published by Graywolf Press, which will publish a new book of poetry, *Moon Crossing Bridge*, as well as reprint her short-story collection, *Lover of Horses*. Another book of poems, *Portable Kisses*, will be coming from Capra Press. Ms. Gallagher has written the introduction to *Carver Country*, a volume of photographs by Bob Adelman that documents her late husband, Raymond Carver's, life and work, as well as an introduction for volumes I and II of the uncollected works of Raymond Carver. She lives in Port Angeles, Washington.

Nikki Giovanni is the author of a number of books, including *Black Feeling, Black Talk, Black Judgment, Night Comes Softly, My House, The Women and the Men, Vacation Time, Those Who Ride the Night Winds*, and *Sacred Cows . . . and Other Edibles*. Ms. Giovanni is the recipient of many awards, including an Honorary Doctorate of Humanities from Wilberforce University, a 1983 YMCA Woman of the Year — Cincinnati Chapter, and the Ohioana Book Award.

Patricia Goedicke has published nine books of poems, most recently *The Tongues We Speak*, one of the *New York Times Book Review*'s eight notable poetry books for 1990. A tenth book, *Paul Bunyan's Bearskin*, is forthcoming from Milkweed in February 1992. Ms. Goedicke is currently teaching poetry in the creative writing program at the University of Montana, where she was selected as the 1991 Distinguished Scholar.

Marilyn Hacker is the author of seven books of poetry, including *Going Back to the River*, published by Random House in 1991, and *The Hang-Glider's Daughter: Selected and New Poems* from Onlywomen Press, also in 1991. She received the National Book Award in 1975 for *Presentation Piece*. Ms. Hacker divides her time between New York, Paris, and Gambier, Ohio, where she is editor of *The Kenyon Review*.

Judith Hemschemeyer is an Associate Professor of English at the University of Central Florida, Orlando. Her books of poems are *I Remember the Room Was Filled with Light*, from Wesleyan, *Very Close and Very Slow*, and *The Ride Home*. Her translations of *The Complete Poems of Anna Akhmatova* were published in 1990 by Zephyr Press, Somerville, Massachusetts.

Sandra Hoben was born in Naugatuck, Connecticut, and educated at St. John's College, Fresno State University, and the University of Utah. Her poems have appeared in *Ironwood*, *Partisan Review*, the *Antioch Review*, and in a chapbook, *Snow Flowers*, from Westigan Press. She teaches with California Poets-in-the-Schools and lives in the San Francisco Bay area with her husband and son.

Sandra Hochman's books include *Manhattan Pastures*, *Voyage Home*, and *Earthworks*.

Jill Hoffman is the author of *Mink Coat* and *Jack Shall Have Jill*. She was a Guggenheim Fellow in poetry from 1974 through 1975.

Colette Inez is the author of *Family Life*, *Eight Minutes from the Sun*, *Alive and Taking Names*, and *The Woman Who Loved Worms*, which received the 1972 Great Lakes Colleges

Association National Book Award. Her *New and Selected Works* is forthcoming, and she is completing *Notes from an Exiled Daughter*, a prose memoir. Her poems are widely anthologized and have appeared in such publications as the *Nation*, the *Yale Review*, the *Hudson Review*, the *New Republic*, *Poetry*, and *Partisan Review*. Born in Brussels, Belgium, she now lives in New York City.

Erica Jong, the author of six novels, including *Fear of Flying*, *How to Save Your Own Life*, and, most recently, *Any Woman's Blues*, has also published five collections of poetry: *Fruits and Vegetables*, *Half-Lives*, *Loveroot*, *At the Edge of the Body*, and *Ordinary Miracles*. Her new and selected poems, *Becoming Light*, were published by HarperCollins in 1991. Ms. Jong has also written a children's book, *Megan's Book of Divorce*, and a nonfiction book called *Witches*.

Shirley Kaufman lives in Jerusalem and is the author of five collections of poetry and several volumes of translations from Hebrew. Her most recent book is *Claims*. Ms. Kaufman won the Alice Fay di Castagnola Award in 1989 and, in 1991, the Shelley Memorial Award of the Poetry Society of America.

Carolyn Kizer is the author of seven books of poetry, one of which, *Yin*, won the Pulitzer Prize in 1985. Her newest book, *The Nearness of You*, was published in 1987.

Maxine Kumin won the Pulitzer Prize for poetry in 1973 for *Up Country* and was consultant in poetry to the Library of Congress from 1981 to 1982. Born in Philadelphia, she was educated at Radcliffe College and now lives in New Hampshire. Ms. Kumin is the author of four novels, eight volumes of poetry, a collection of essays on country living, and a collection of short stories. She has taught at several universities, including Washington University, Brandeis, Columbia, and Princeton.

Denise Levertov was born in 1923 in England to Russian-Jewish and Welsh parents. She published her first book, *The Double Image*, in England in 1946. She has taught at various colleges, including CCNY, Berkeley, and MIT. Among her many volumes of poetry are *With Eyes at the Back of Our Heads, The Jacob's Ladder, O Taste and See, The Sorrow Dance, Relearning the Alphabet, To Stay Alive, Breathing the Water,* and *Oblique Prayers*.

Lyn Lifshin is the author of many books of poetry, including *The Children Who Made It to the Cambodian Border, Upstate Madonna, Black Apples, Kiss the Skin Off, The Doctor Poems, Offered by Owner, Reading Lips,* and *Not Made of Glass,* a collection of poems that accompanies a documentary film of the same name by Karista Press, distributed by Women Make Movies. Ms. Lifshin has edited several collections of women's writing, including an earlier edition of *Tangled Vines; Ariadne's Thread,* a collection of women's diaries and journals from Harper and Row; and *Lips Unsealed,* a collection of women's confidences from Capra Press. She gives readings and workshops and lectures all over the country.

Audre Lorde is the author of *The First Cities, Cables to Rage, Coal, Burst of Light,* and *Our Dead Behind Us.* In 1991 she was named state poet of New York.

Mary Makofske teaches writing workshops at Orange County Community College, Middletown, New York. She is the author of *The Disappearance of Gargoyles* and winner of the 1991 Robert Penn Warren Poetry Prize, sponsored by *Cumberland* poetry review. Her poems have appeared in *G.W. Review*, *Calyx*, *Slant*, *Wordsmith*, *Zone 3*, and *Blue Unicorn*.

Judith McDaniel, a poet and prose writer, is the author of *Sanctuary: a Journey* and *Metamorphosis*.

Heather McHugh is the author of *Because the Sea Is Black* and *Shades*. She lives in Eastport, Maine, and is, she says, learning the ropes with a teenage stepdaughter.

Judith Minty is the author of six books of poetry. Her first book, *Lake Songs and Other Fears*, was the recipient of the United States Award of the International Poetry Forum in 1973. Her most recent collection, *Dancing the Fault*, was published by the University of Central Florida Press. Ms. Minty is originally from the Great Lakes region of Michigan, but now lives in a fishing village in Northern California and teaches at Humboldt State University. She also writes fiction.

Honor Moore's poems have been widely published in journals and anthologies, and a collection, *Memoir*, was published by Chicory Blue Press in 1988. Her verse play *Mourning Pictures* was produced on Broadway, as well as in San Francisco, Minneapolis, and London. She has received a fellowship in playwriting from the New York State Council on the Arts and in poetry from the NEA. Ms. Moore lives in northwestern Connecticut, where she is completing a biography of her grandmother, the painter Margaret Sargent, to be published in 1993.

Sharon Olds is the author of several books of poetry, the most recent being *The Gold Cell*, published by Knopf in 1987. Ms. Olds presently teaches at Columbia, New York University, and Goldwater Hospital on Roosevelt Island.

Alicia Ostriker is the author of seven books of poetry, one of which, *Stealing the Language: The Emergence of Women's Poetry in America*, has been hailed as a critical landmark. She has received awards from the NEA, the Guggenheim Foundation, the Rockefeller Foundation, and the Poetry Society of America. Ms. Ostriker teaches English and creative writing at Rutgers University.

Linda Pastan has published seven volumes of poetry, including *A Perfect Circle of Sun*, *Aspects of Eve*, *The Five Stages of Grief*, *The Imperfect Paradise*, and *Heroes in Disguise*. She is the recipient of the Dylan Thomas Award, a Pushcart Prize, the Alice Fay Di Castagnola Award, the Bess Hopkin Prize, and the Maurice English Award. Ms. Pastan is on the Bread Loaf Writers' Conference and has taught at the American University. In 1991 she was appointed poet laureate of Maryland.

Molly Peacock is the author of three books of poems, *Take Heart* and *Raw Heaven*, both from Random House, and *And Live Apart*, from the University of Missouri Press. Her poems have appeared in the *New Yorker*, the *Nation*, the *Paris*

Review, and *Poetry*. Among her grants and awards are an NEA fellowship, two fellowships from the Ingram Merrill Foundation, and three fellowships from the New York Foundation for the Arts. She has been visiting professor at a number of universities, including New York University, Barnard, Columbia, Sarah Lawrence, and Hofstra. A learning specialist in private practice as well as at Friends Seminary, Ms. Peacock lives in New York City and serves as president of the Poetry Society of America.

Marge Piercy has published a number of books of poetry and fiction, and recently edited *Early Ripening*, an anthology of poetry by women writing today. *Available Light*, her most recent collection of poetry, was published by Knopf.

Sylvia Plath, born in Boston in 1932, was living in Devon, England, at the time of her death in 1963. Her books of poetry include *Ariel*, *The Colossus*, *Crossing the Water*, and *Winter Trees*. Ms. Plath is the author of *The Bell Jar* and a children's book, *The Bed Book*.

Adrienne Rich has written many books of poetry, including *Change of World*, *The Diamond Cutters*, *Leaflets*, *The Will to Change*, *Time's Power: Poems 1985–88*, and *Your Native Land, Your Life*. Her first book of poems, *Change of World*, received the Yale Younger Poets Award in 1951.

Sonia Sanchez was born in Birmingham, Alabama, and is the author of twelve books, including *Homecoming*, *We a BaddDDD People*, *Love Poems*, *I've Been a Woman: New and Selected Poems*, *A Sound Investment and Other Stories*, and

Homegirls and Handgrenades. In addition to being a contributing editor to *Black Scholar* and the *Journal of African Studies*, Ms. Sanchez has edited two anthologies, *We Be Word Sorcerers: 25 Stories by Black Americans* and *360° of Blackness Coming at You.* She is professor of English at Temple University.

Anne Sexton was born in 1928 in Newton, Massachusetts. Her poetry has appeared in virtually every major magazine in the United States, and she received a Pulitzer Prize in 1967 for her poetry collection *Live or Die.* Ms. Sexton's other books include *To Bedlam and Part Way Back, The Death Notebooks,* and *The Awful Rowing Toward God.* A professor at Boston University, Ms. Sexton died in 1974.

Kathleen Spivack has published poetry in the *New Yorker, Poetry,* the *Atlantic Monthly,* and the *Paris Review,* and her books include *Flying Inland* and *The Jane Poems,* from Doubleday, *Swimmer in the Spreading Dawn,* from Applewood Books, *The Beds We Lie In,* from Scarecrow, and *The Honeymoon,* a collection of short stories from Graywolf Press. Among her numerous awards are grants from the NEA and the Bunting Institute and a Discovery award. Currently, Ms. Spivack is visiting professor of American poetry at the University of Paris.

Janet Sternburg was born in Boston, Massachusetts, and received a degree in philosophy from the New School for Social Research in New York. A poet and essayist, as well as a writer for theater and film, she has a special interest in women and creativity and has edited the first two volumes of a collection of essays on being a woman and a writer, titled *The Writer and Her Work*. She is currently acting as curator for a television series of films by women as well as working on a collection of her personal essays.

Karen Swenson was born in New York City and attended Barnard College. She has taught at City College, and has been poet-in-residence at Clark University, Skidmore College, University of Idaho, Denver University, and Scripps College. Her first book, *An Attic of Ideals*, was published by Doubleday in 1974. A subsequent chapbook, *East-West*, was published by Confluence Press in 1980. Ms. Swenson's work has been published in the *New Yorker*, the *Nation*, *Saturday Review*, *American Poetry Review*, and *Prairie Schooner*, among other journals, and she has been a fellow at both the Bread Loaf and Yaddo conferences. She spends part of each year in southeast Asia.

Abigail Thomas has had fiction published in the *Missouri Review*, the *Little Magazine*, and *Columbine*, and has published poetry in the *Paris Review*.

Gail Todd, the daughter of Jewish immigrants, grew up in a housing project in the Bronx. Her book of poems, *Family Way*, was published by Shameless Hussy Press. Ms. Todd works as a technical writer and lives in Berkeley, California, with her husband and two children.

Patricia Traxler, the author of *Blood Calendar*, from William Morrow, and *The Glass Woman*, from Hanging Loose, was Bunting poetry fellow at Radcliffe from 1990 to 1991. She is working on her third volume of poetry and recently completed a novel, *Earthly Luck*. Ms. Traxler received the Cohen Award from *Ploughshares* in 1990.

Liv Ullmann is an internationally known actress and the author of *Changing*.

Diane Wakoski has been writer-in-residence since 1975 at Michigan State University, where she has been made university distinguished professor. She is the author of sixteen collections of poems; *Medea the Sorceress*, the most recent, is the first volume of a long poem of the West entitled the *Archaebology of Movies and Books*.

Anne Waldman, a poet, performer, and lecturer, has published ten books of poetry, including *Blue Mosque*, *Skin Meat Bones*, and *First Baby Poems*. She toured with Bob Dylan's Rolling Thunder Review and performed in Dylan's film *Renaldo and Clara*. Ms. Waldman, who performs her poetry from coast to coast, was assistant director of the Poetry Project at St. Mark's Church in the Bowery and founder and codirector of the Jack Kerouac School of Disembodied Poetics, the Naropa Institute.

Alice Walker, poet, novelist, short-story writer, and essayist, has received the Pulitzer Prize, the PEN/Freedom to Write Award, and the American Book Award. Her books include two collections of short stories, *In Love and Trouble* and *You Can't Keep a Good Woman Down*, and five volumes of poetry, *Once*; *Revolutionary Petunias*; *Goodnight, Willie Lee, I'll See You in the Morning*; *Horses Make a Landscape Look More Beautiful*; and *Her Blue Body Everything We Know*. Ms. Walker has also published two essay collections, *In Search of*

Our Mothers' Gardens and *Living by the Word*, two children's books, a biography of Langston Hughes, and four novels: *The Third Life of Grange Copeland*, *Meridian*, *The Color Purple*, and *The Temple of My Familiar*.

Dara Wier's books include *The Eight Step Grape Vine*, *All You Have In Common*, *The Book of Knowledge*, and most recently, *Blue for the Plough*.

Ellen Wittlinger's book of poems, *Breakers*, was published by the Sheep Meadow Press in 1979. Since then she has had five plays performed in Boston or New York. The mother of two, she is currently the children's librarian in Swampscot, Massachusetts, where she is completing work on two novels.

Yvonne is a poet and filmmaker. The poetry editor at *Ms.* from 1973 to 1986, she is the author of two full-length books of poetry, *Iwilla/Soil* and *Iwilla/Scourge*, as well as a chapbook, *Iwilla*. She has received several poetry awards, including the Brio Award in 1991, as well as grants from the NEA in 1974 and 1984, a Mary Roberts Rinehart grant in 1974, and a New York State CAPS grant in 1981.

Lila Zeiger's work has been published widely since her first three poems appeared in the *Paris Review* in the late 1970s. She is the author of *The Way to Castle Garden*, from State Street Press, and is now completing a book of short stories. Ms. Zeiger's awards include a Witter Brynner grant for 1990 through 1991, and a New York State CAPS grant in poetry.

Acknowledgments

We are grateful to the following poets, publishers, and copyright holders for permission to include the poems in this volume:

ELLEN BASS: "For My Mother" and "First Menstruation," copyright © 1977 by Ellen Bass. Reprinted from *Of Separateness and Merging* by permission of the author.

OLGA BROUMAS: "Little Red Riding Hood," reprinted by permission of the author.

SIV CEDERING: "Poem for My Mother," copyright © 1976 by Siv Cedering. Reprinted from *Calliopea Press Post Card* by permission of the author.

LUCILLE CLIFTON: "My Mama moved among the days," from *Good Woman: Poems and a Memoir 1969–1980*, copyright © 1987 by Lucille Clifton. Reprinted by permission of BOA Editions, Ltd., 92 Park Avenue, Brockport, NY 14420, and the author.

WANDA COLEMAN: "Dear Mama (4)," reprinted by permission of the author.

TOI DERRICOTTE: "Christmas Eve: My Mother Dressing" and "Touching/Not Touching: My Mother," reprinted from *Captivity*, University of Pittsburgh Press, 1989, by permission of the author.

DIANE DI PRIMA: "Letter to Jeanne," copyright 1976 by Diane di Prima. Reprinted from *Selected Poems: 1956–1975* by permission of the author.